The Guided Construction of Knowledge

Multilingual Matters

Please contact us for the latest book information:
Multilingual Matters Ltd, Frankfurt Lodge, Clevedon Hall,
Victoria Road, Clevedon, Avon BS21 7SJ, England.

The Guided Construction of Knowledge

Talk Amongst Teachers and Learners

Neil Mercer

MULTILINGUAL MATTERS LTD
Clevedon • Philadelphia • Adelaide

Library of Congress Cataloging in Publication Data

Mercer, Neil
The Guided Construction of Knowledge: Talk Amongst Teachers and
Learners/Neil Mercer
Includes bibliographical references and index
1. Communication in education. 2. Knowledge, Theory of. 3. Children–
language. 4. Learning, Psychology of. 5. Interaction analysis in education.
I. Title.
LB1033.b.M37   1995
371.1'022–dc20   94-25144

British Library Cataloguing in Publication Data

A CIP catalogue record for this book is available from the British Library.

ISBN 1-85359-263-3 (hbk)
ISBN 1-85359-262-5 (pbk)

Multilingual Matters Ltd

UK: Frankfurt Lodge, Clevedon Hall, Victoria Road, Clevedon, Avon BS21 7SJ.
USA: 1900 Frost Road, Suite 101, Bristol, PA 19007, USA.
Australia: P.O. Box 6025, 83 Gilles Street, Adelaide, SA 5000, Australia.

Index compiled by Isobel McLean (Society of Indexers).
Printed and bound in Great Britain by the Cromwell Press.

Contents

Contents

Preface

This book has emerged from research carried out over the last ten or so years, in schools and other places, on the process of teaching and learning through talk. Others as well as myself were involved, directly or indirectly, in this research. I draw a great deal on their ideas (but I may not do proper justice to them). I am thinking here particularly of Derek Edwards, Jo Longman, Karen Littleton, Janet Maybin, Andy Northedge, Barry Stierer, Joan Swann, Rupert Wegerif and the SLANT project team (John Elliott, Eunice Fisher, Terry Phillips and Peter Scrimshaw). I have also had the benefit of the comments of some of those people on earlier drafts of this book, for which I am eternally grateful. For other very constructive conversations I thank Douglas Barnes, Rib Davis, Sylvia Rojas-Drummond, Paul Light, Mark Prentice, Harold Rosen and Madeline Watson. To Lyn Dawes, as teacher-researcher, critical reader and supportive friend, my gratitude is beyond expression.

Without the co-operation of teachers and pupils in schools in various parts of England, and especially in Watling Way Middle School in Milton Keynes, this book could not have been written and I offer them my heartfelt thanks. Without the able support of Pam Powter, CLAC secretary, the work of writing this book would have been immensely greater and much more stressful. Finally, I gratefully acknowledge the financial support for my research provided by the Economic and Social Research Council in grants to two projects, *The Development of Understanding in the Classroom* (Ref. C00232236) and *Spoken Language and New Technology* (Ref. R000232731).

Transcriptions

Chapters 2–6 of the book contain many transcribed episodes of speech. Those which are numbered and titled (such as *Sequence 5.1: History in the Making*) were recorded by me or come from research in which I was directly involved. Generally speaking, the chapters are organised around these numbered sequences. I have tried to present my own transcriptions in a non-technical way, so as to make them accessible to audiences outside the community of language researchers who are used to reading transcripts.

This means that I have only included such information about pauses, overlapping speech, pronunciation, emphasis and other non-verbal aspects of communication as I thought absolutely necessary in the circumstances. If some readers miss such detail, I apologise. I have also been glad to be able to include many illustrative transcripts from other people's research, and acknowledge them accordingly in the text.

For more information about the methods of analysis I use, I refer readers to the 'Appendix' by Janet Maybin in D. Edwards and N. Mercer (1987) *Common Knowledge* (London: Methuen/Routledge); to N. Mercer (1991) Researching common knowledge: studying the content and context of educational discourse, in G. Walford (ed.) *Doing Educational Research* (London: Routledge); and to N. Mercer (1995) Socio-cultural perspectives and the study of classroom discourse, in C. Coll (ed.) *Classroom Discourse* (Madrid: Infancia y Aprendizaje).

1 What the Book is About

This book is about a communication process which is common and important in all societies, that in which one person helps another to develop their knowledge and understanding. It is at the heart of what we call 'education' (though education involves much more) and it combines both 'teaching' and 'learning' (which we tend to talk about as if they were two separate processes). There is no precise name for it in English, and so I call it 'the guided construction of knowledge'. I am interested in this process wherever it takes place, and especially in how it happens in the classrooms of schools and other educational establishments. In this book, I try to describe this process by analysing the language of real-life events — talk between teachers and learners, or between learners who are working together. My analysis of the talk is based on a particular view of the relationship between language and thought, which I will begin to explain in this chapter.

If you try to pin down what is meant by 'knowledge', you may conclude that you are dealing with something that is located in individual people's heads. Of course, knowledge exists in the thought of individual people. But to think of it only as an individual mental possession does not do justice to it, or to the capabilities of human beings. Knowledge is also a joint possession, because it can very effectively be shared. What one human being discovers — how to get from town A to town B, how light travels through space, how it feels to fall in love — can be made available to others (as shown by the evident and continued success of cartography, physics and popular music). We do not each have to reinvent the wheel. But another important quality of human endeavour, often overlooked in the study of learning and problem-solving, is that amongst all living things we are uniquely equipped to pool our mental resources and solve problems — to create knowledge — through joint mental effort. In *Common Knowledge*, which I wrote with Derek Edwards, we used our observations of lessons in some primary schools to show how teachers and pupils went about this. But the guided construction of knowledge is not something that happens only in schools. The history of ideas shows that discovery, learning and creative problem-solving are rarely, if ever, truly individual affairs. All

1

creative thinkers, even those singled out for individual acclaim in the histories of the world , have worked with others and with the ideas of others as well as their own. Indeed, some of the most successful individuals in their fields have been visibly part of a collective endeavour which seemed to raise the quality of each individual contribution (the Impressionists, the Bloomsbury group, the Beatles…). Two heads *are* often better than one, and one result of a great many heads contributing to the construction of knowledge is the vast dynamic resource of knowledge we call 'culture'.

However, the process of sharing knowledge and developing under-standing often seems to go awry. People misunderstand each other, teachers teach badly, students transform sensible ideas into nonsense. But the failures are as important for our understanding of the process as the successes, and they may also be better understood by looking carefully at the talk that generates them. In societies across the world, some people — notably parents, teachers and trainers — are vested with a particular responsibility for the process of helping others develop knowledge and understanding. They are expected to provide a new generation with access to existing knowledge and equip them with the tools for advancing it. They act out this responsibility in many ways, but the most obvious way is by talking with learners.

Ask yourself why schoolteachers talk to children. One obvious reason is so that they can tell children what to do, how to do it, when to start and when to stop. But of course teachers do much more. They assess children's learning through talking to children and listening to what they say; they provide children with educational experiences which would be hard to provide by any means other than talk (e.g. telling stories, reading poetry, describing and explaining events, supplying factual information at the right time and in an accessible form). And, of course, teachers use talk to control the behaviour of children.[1] There has been a good deal of educational research on this. Here, however, I am more interested in how talk is used to shape representations of reality and interpretations of experience.

A Socio-Cultural Psychology

One element of the guided construction of knowledge is 'learning'. Like all human endeavours, the process of learning can be examined from more than one perspective. Of course, this is true of all phenomena; how you study something as seemingly unambiguous as 'the ocean' will depend on what your interests are (the life cycles of fish, the effects of global warming, the routes of merchant shipping…?) and how you define it (does your definition include all interconnected seas...?). However, 'learning' does not even exist somewhere out there to the same extent as 'the ocean'. Psychologists who study learning are doing so in order to learn; they are studying the very thing they are engaged in doing. This makes it even more difficult to separate the phenomenon — the thing being studied — from the methods used to study it.

In the history of psychology, topics like 'learning' and 'problem-solving' have typically been defined as processes which go on inside the head of each individual person. They have therefore usually been studied by designing experiments in which isolated individuals perform tasks set by a researcher, who gives the subject instructions and gathers data objectively from observing their performance. For example, ever since the German psychologist Hermann Ebbinghaus invented 'nonsense syllables' (things like 'wak', 'cef', 'gur') in the late nineteenth century, an army of experimenters has compared and contrasted people's ability to learn and recall them under a variety of carefully controlled conditions. In this classic tradition of experimental psychology, each experimental subject is seen merely as an individual representative of the human race, being studied objectively by scientists.[2] But think for a minute about what is going in such events and you will see that they can be conceived of in quite a different way. Any such psychological experiment is a kind of conversation, in which two people strive for a new level of understanding. The experimenter has to explain clearly to the subject how to perform the task, perhaps also persuade the subject that there is nothing to fear from doing it; they may also wish the subject to know that they are very grateful for the time he or she is giving. The subject may need to ask questions about the task and may have to provide responses to it in words. At the end of the conversation, some knowledge will have been shared. The subject may have learned very little of value, while the experimenter may have learned something very useful; but that is another issue. The point is that even the study of learning as an individual process involves talk and joint activity. However, most psychological research on learning has not regarded this as very important. Dialogues between researcher and subject are normally treated simply as aspects of experimental method ('subjects were given the following instructions about how to do the task...') and not seen as part of the object of study. That is, the analysis of the communicative process whereby the experiment was set up and the data were collected usually falls outside the scope of the researcher's theory of learning or problem-solving. Yet there is now a lot of evidence, especially from the study of children's cognitive development, that the performance of subjects in experimental tasks is strongly affected by what the experimenter actually says to them and their subsequent interpretation of what they are meant to do.[3]

An alternative perspective on the study of the development of knowledge and understanding is one which gives more explicit recognition to the role of language as a means for constructing knowledge and understanding. It redefines the topic of enquiry, which becomes not 'learning' but instead 'teaching-and-learning'. It studies how people use language as *a social mode of thinking*. It treats knowledge as something which is socially constructed, and so has become known as the *socio-cultural* approach. As you will no doubt have gathered, this is the approach that I will be taking, and I will describe it in most detail in Chapter 5.

Language as a Social Mode of Thinking

By describing language as a social mode of thinking, I can draw attention to two important ways in which language is related to thought. One is that language is a vital means by which we represent our own thoughts to ourselves. The Russian psychologist Vygotsky[4] described language as a *psychological tool*, something each of us uses to make sense of experience. Language is also our essential *cultural tool* — we use it to share experience and so to collectively, jointly, make sense of it. Language is a means for transforming experience into cultural knowledge and understanding. It is mainly through the medium of spoken and written language that successive generations of a society benefit from the experience of the past, and it is also language that each new generation uses to share, dispute and define its own experience. Language is therefore not just a means by which individuals can formulate ideas and communicate them, it is also a means for people to think and learn together.

So although it is useful to describe language as having these two functions, its cultural function (communicating) and its psychological one (thinking) are not really separate. At the simplest level, whenever you talk, you have to think what to say, and think about what you hear. You may spend some time thinking about what people have said, what you said yourself and what you might say on future occasions. And some of the most creative thinking takes place when people are talking together (hence the popularity of 'brainstorming' as a creative technique). One of the opportunities school can offer pupils[5] is the chance to involve other people in their thoughts — to use conversations to develop their own thoughts. Look, for example, at the following conversation between two seven-year-olds, Mel and Chris, who are trying to write an eye-witness account of the Nativity

Story (they are sitting in the classroom, in front of the computer on which they are going to write their story):

Mel: What they'd be doing?
They'd be doing what?

Chris: They could be doing like things some feeding their donkey they had in their back garden.

Mel: Oh no we could put, they could, their father could have drawed a hop-scotch so the girl was playing on the hop-scotch and the boy was...

Chris: Playing what?

Mel: Or they might just be sitting in the house reading a book or something.

Chris: I know, they're outside and they're getting suntanned.

Mel: Yes cos Bethlehem's a hot place. 'Once', let's put 'Once in Bethlehem...'

Chris: That would be good wouldn't it? (*They turn to the computer and Chris reaches out to the keyboard.*)[6]

We can see here how the children use language to leap from one creative image to another, and to evaluate the possibilities as they are presented. From a very early age, children use language to formulate ideas and evaluate them. When children are two or three years old, you can often hear them talking aloud, alone, for their own benefit. (Both Piaget and Vygotsky called this 'egocentric speech'.)[7] But the distinction between 'what you say to yourself' and 'what you say to someone else' is to some extent a matter of social learning, a convention which most of us learn and choose to abide by to avoid the label of eccentricity or madness. (People who live solitary lives often let this convention slip.) As children grow out of infancy, you can find increasingly in their speech remarks which are hard to define as 'egocentric speech' or 'communicative speech', perhaps because they have more than one function. When my daughter Anna was nearly three, she was often insistent that I take part in her games. As with all parents, however, my stamina was limited. One day, when we had already spent a lot of time together, I encouraged her to play alone while I read the paper. She did this for a while and then began the following non-conversation:

Anna: Daddy, will you play with me?
(*no reply*)

Anna: Daddy will you play with me?
(*no reply*)

Anna: Daddy! Daddy will you play? (*pause*) She said to her daddy.

I cannot tell if her final remark was meant for my ears, but it did gain

my attention. By saying 'She said to her Daddy' she effectively placed her
own previous remark in inverted commas. She gave her own utterance the
status of dialogue in a story. Anna appeared to be reflecting her cultural
experience as a listener in her performance as a speaker, not in the simple
and obvious sense of becoming able to say words that she had heard
someone else say, but by using her past experience of another kind of
language event (being read a story) to recast, to redefine — to re*think* — her
current experience. For an instant, she took on the voice of the storyteller
of her own life. Another way of putting this is to say that Anna *appropriated*[8]
the language of her story books and story tapes, and used it to see herself
from 'outside' herself, as a little girl with a daddy. We can glimpse here, as
in the language experience of each of us, how the psychological and
communicative functions of language are intimately related.

Through conversations with parents, teachers and other 'guides', we
acquire ways of using language that can reshape our thoughts. Language
is something we acquire as part of growing up in the company of others,
and the language carries with it the cultural knowledge of a community.
But language does not just carry or represent the knowledge of our culture;
the ways we talk and write are themselves part of that cultural knowledge.
In this sense, the image of language as a 'tool' is misleading, because tools
are normally ready-made, given objects that are picked up and used to do
a job and are unchanged in the process. Language is not like that. By using
language to learn, we may change the language we use. This is why an
analysis of the process of teaching and learning, of constructing knowledge,
must be an analysis of language in use.

A Summary of the Rest of the Book

In Chapter 2, I use examples of people helping other people to learn to
illustrate what I mean by 'the guided construction of knowledge' as it
happens in schools and other places. I argue that we need to see classrooms
as one of a range of distinctive settings in which knowledge is jointly
constructed and in which some people help others to develop their
understanding.

In Chapter 3, one of my main aims is to show how the ways teachers use
language can be analysed and evaluated in social context. In every society,
people who are responsible for guiding the construction of knowledge do
so by using certain kinds of guidance strategies, and these include certain
language *techniques* which are commonly used by teachers for developing
a shared version of educational knowledge with their students. I describe

some of these techniques and use classroom examples to illustrate them and to consider how well they fit their intended purpose.

Chapter 4 looks at how learners respond to the guidance of their teachers and actively influence the course of teaching and learning events. Learners are constrained, in the ways they are expected to talk and act, by their relationship with their teacher; but there are also many ways that learners influence what their teachers say and do.

Chapter 5 is a sketch for a theory of how talk is used to guide the construction of knowledge in schools and other educational institutions. By 'theory' I mean something very practical and useful — a simplified, explanatory model of the process of teaching and learning as it is carried out through talk in classrooms. We do not yet have a satisfactory theory of this process, in my opinion, though research has provided some excellent resources for building one. Later in the chapter, I list what I believe are the essential requirements for this theory and suggest how these requirements can be met.

In Chapter 6, I look at how learners use talk and joint activity to construct knowledge in the classroom, by working together without the continuous presence of a teacher. There has been a good deal of research on 'collaborative learning' in recent years, which I review and relate to concepts introduced in earlier chapters. I use my own and other research to typify certain ways of talking, ways that represent different social modes of thinking. I then go on to suggest how students can be helped to achieve a better understanding, appreciation and use of talk for constructing knowledge.

The final, brief chapter of the book is a personal perspective on the future of research on the guided construction of knowledge in schools.

Notes

1. See, for example, Chapter 2 of Edwards, A.D. and Westgate, D. (1987) *Investigating Classroom Talk*. London: The Falmer Press.
2. For a socio-cultural criticism of the Ebbinghaus tradition of experimental psychology, see Säljö, R. (1992) Human growth and the complex society: Notes on the monocultural bias in theories of learning. *Cultural Dynamics* 5 (1), 43–56.
3. For a discussion of the relationship between experimenters and child-subjects in psychological research, see Elbers, E. (1991) The development of competence in its social context. *Educational Psychology Review* 3 (2), 73–93, and the articles in that issue which follow it. Also, Light, P. and Perret-Clermont, A-N. (1989) Social context effects in learning and testing. In A. Gellatly, D. Rogers and J. Sloboda (eds) *Cognition and Social Worlds*. Oxford: Clarendon Press.
4. Vygotsky, L.S. (1978) *Mind in Society*. London: Harvard University Press.

5. I use the terms 'pupil' and 'student' more or less interchangeably throughout the book, and also the term 'learner' where it seems most appropriate.

6. This conversation is taken from page 248 of Fisher, E. (1993) Distinctive features of pupil–pupil classroom talk and their relationship to learning: How discursive exploration might be encouraged. *Language and Education* 7 (4), 239–57. It is part of the data of the Spoken Language and New Technology (SLANT) research project, in which I was involved and which is described in more detail in Chapter 6.

7. Piaget, J. (1926) *The Language and Thought of the Child*. New York: Harcourt Brace Jovanovich. Vygotsky, L.S. (1962) *Thought and Language*. Cambridge, MA: MIT Press.

8. This meaning of 'appropriation' was apparently coined by one of Vygotsky's colleagues, Leont'ev (Leont'ev, A.N. (1981) *Problems of the Development of Mind*. Moscow: Progress Publishers). As it is usually applied in early childhood research, 'appropriation' is concerned with what meanings children may take from encounters with objects in cultural context. Because humans are essentially cultural beings, even young children's initial encounters with objects are inevitably cultural experiences. If they first encounter a tool like a hammer when it is being used, then the meaning of that object for them will include its function in their community and not just its physical characteristics. In relation to schooling, the most interesting application of the concept will not necessarily concern objects, but rather *language* and the representation of concepts and ideas. See also Newman, D., Griffin, P. and Cole, M. (1989) *The Construction Zone*. Cambridge: Cambridge University Press; Mercer, N. (1992) Culture, context, and the construction of knowledge in the classroom. In P. Light and G. Butterworth (eds) *Context and Cognition: Ways of Learning and Knowing*. Hemel Hempstead: Harvester-Wheatsheaf.

2 Ways of Talking

The main aim of this chapter is to provide some examples of people helping other people to learn and so illustrate what I mean by 'the guided construction of knowledge'. In later chapters I will concentrate mainly on events in schools, but the examples here show teaching and learning going on in some other places too. While the process of formal education has some special characteristics which we need to take account of, I believe that it is also useful to see classrooms as just one of a range of real-life settings in which knowledge is jointly constructed and in which some people help others to develop their understanding.

The first sequence is from the very first driving lesson given by an aunt (Marie) to her teenage niece (Rebecca). They are sitting in Marie's car, with Rebecca behind the wheel.

Sequence 2.1: A driving lesson

Marie:	Right. You have to know where everything is first. Umm.
Rebecca:	Umm, yeh.
Marie:	Right, do you know what the footpedals are for? No?
Rebecca:	Yeh but I can't remember which way it goes.
Marie:	It goes, um, that one on the right, accelerator. (*R presses it*) Yeh.
Rebecca:	Yeh, accelerator, brake, clutch, ABC.
Marie:	That's right. yeh. So you move that foot from one to the other, so you can't have it on both, right? Do you know what the clutch is for?
Rebecca:	Change gears.
Marie:	Right, go on then, try changing gears without the engine switched on. Put your foot on the clutch and…
Rebecca:	(*interrupting, looking at the gearstick*) Where are they? It hasn't got any numbers.
Marie:	Yeh, you're right. I think it is here (*points to the faded numbers*). Look, but they're invisible. 1, 2, cross (*she moves the stick as she speaks*) 3, 4, cross, 5 and reverse. So you want to be as far as

possible across this way and up, for 1. (*R takes the gearstick*) Across towards me. Will it not go? Take it back to the middle again. Make it wobble. That's it, try 2, 3, 4 and 5. Now reverse, you have to lift it.

Rebecca: Lift it?

Marie: Lift (*R does it*) and across, that's it. Right. Right. So you can't put it in reverse by mistake. Reverse has got to be a real thing. [*and a little later*]

Marie: Which of the dials would you know what they mean, so that I don't have to tell you?

Rebecca: That one (*points to speedometer*).

Marie: Yeh, shows how fast you go. Right, now that one.

Rebecca: I know it means 'revs', but I don't know what they mean.

Marie: I don't think many people do.

Rebecca: Revelations?

Marie: Revelations! (*laughs*) That's a book of the Bible. It's 'revolutions'. It's how much it's going round, the bits in the engine, it mustn't go over the red.

At this early stage, learning to drive is mainly a matter of familiarisation with equipment and procedures. Understandably, Marie does a lot of straightforward informing and instructing. But she also asks questions of a certain kind — ones to which she already knows the answer — because she wants and needs to know what Rebecca already knows. To be effective, any teacher needs to explore the scope of a learner's existing knowledge. Through Rebecca's own contributions (e.g. 'accelerator, brake, clutch, ABC') it becomes apparent that she already has some relevant knowledge. This probably encourages Marie to ask more questions (e.g. 'Do you know what the clutch is for?') rather than simply telling Rebecca about the rest of the controls. So through this process (a) Rebecca not only gains new knowledge, but gets the opportunity to check, refine and elaborate what she already knows; and (b) Marie learns about what Rebecca knows and what she can do and is able to adjust her teaching strategy accordingly.

I have concentrated here on the talk, but in learning a skill like driving, the non-verbal activity (e.g. pointing to and manipulating the controls) is an essential, integral part of the process. In fact, much of the rest of this lesson proceeded through a process that Barbara Rogoff calls 'guided participation', in which words are used to direct actions and to provide encouragement and feedback on the consequences. In her book *Apprenticeship in Thinking*,[1] Rogoff provides some good examples of parents teaching their young children in this way. Language is important in such situations, but so is the involvement of both the teacher and learner in joint physical activity. In much of the academic teaching and learning that I will be dealing with later in the book, language is rather more important. Learning to drive is essentially a matter of learning procedures, motor skills and developing suitably rapid physical responses to events. But a lot of the learning we do in the world of education is a matter of learning ways of using language itself.

The next sequence comes from an occasion when Antonia, a child of 3, was sitting in the back of a car with her older sister Kay (14 years). It was a long journey, and Kay had been amusing Antonia by singing 'The Alphabet Song' with her. Kay then encouraged her to recite numbers in the same way:

Sequence 2.2: Paired counting

Antonia:	I do one first. No you do one first.
Kay:	OK. One.
Antonia:	Two.
Kay:	Three.
	(*and so on up to...*)
Kay:	fifteen.
Antonia:	seventeen.
Kay:	sixteen! Yours is sixteen.
Antonia:	sixteen.
Kay:	seventeen.
Antonia:	eighteen.
Kay:	nineteen.
Antonia:	tenteen.
Kay:	No! (*laughs*) Twenty.
Antonia:	Twenty.
Kay:	Twenty-one. Keep going.

Here we can see Kay helping Antonia to do something which she would not otherwise have been quite able to do — count up to twenty-one. Kay initiates the activity, but Antonia (drawing on some experience of playing it before) defines who should begin. Kay obviously knows all the answers, and for this activity it is essential that one person does. The regular structure of the interaction simplifies the task of counting for Antonia, and enables Kay to support Antonia's efforts. Chanting games like this are used in many societies for teaching children basic information which can be represented as a list or series. The participants also have a self-awareness about their respective states of knowledge which is essential for the game to work as a teaching–learning event. Antonia knows that Kay knows all the numbers, and that she doesn't (quite) know them herself. She accepts, without question, Kay's corrections. The activity therefore is an *acting out* of their different states of knowledge, with the probable outcome that Antonia's competence in reciting numbers is improved each time the 'game' is played.

Next I want to look at part of a discussion which was captured by a teacher in a south London school who left a tape recorder running while a group of girls (aged 11 and 12) worked together on a maths problem. The problem was this:

> You have a square sheet of card measuring 15 cm by 15 cm and you want to use it to make an open cuboid container by cutting out the corners. What is the maximum capacity the container can have?

For our purposes here, it is useful to focus on one of the four girls, called Emily in the transcript (the other girls are represented as A, B and C). Emily was considered by her teacher to be quite confident and able in mathematics. At the point the transcript begins, the girls have made a box to the dimensions required out of card marked out in centimetre squares, but Emily is unhappy that the box seems to have got 'bigger' despite having lost its corners. This is because she has a fundamental misunderstanding about what they are doing. As you read, try to work out what her difficulty is.

Sequence 2.3: Maximum Box

Emily: This box is bigger than what it should be 'cos if you get 15 by 15 you get 225, but if you times um 9 by 9 times 3 you still get 243 and I haven't got that much space in my box.

A: You have.

Emily: But the 15 by…

B: It can be, it can work, I think.

Emily: But surely…

B: You cut off corners.

Emily: Yeh but that surely should make it *smaller*.

B: I think that is right.

Emily: (*counting squares marked on the paper*) Hang on, 1,2,3,4,5…

C: You're not going to get 243.

Emily: I shouldn't get 243 'cos if the piece of paper only had 225 then, um…

C: Hang on, look…9 times 9 times how many was it up?

A: But don't you remember, Emily, it's got all this space in the middle.

Emily: Yeh, but…

A: It's got all that space in the middle.

C: It is right, Emily, it is, it should be that number.

Emily: But if I have a piece of paper with 225 squares, why should I get more?

A: Because you have all that space in the middle.

Emily: (*sounding exasperated*) No, it hasn't got anything to do with it. If my piece of paper had only 225 squares on it, I can't get more out of the same piece of paper.

A: You can because you're forgetting, things go *up* as well, not just the flat piece of paper like that.

Emily: Oh yeh.

A: It's going up.

C: It's going up.

C: It's because, look, down here you've got 3 and it's going up.

A: You're going 3 up, it's getting more on it. Do you see it will be 243?

Emily: Yeh.

C: It is right, it should be.[2]

In Sequence 2.3 there is no-one who is in the formal role of a teacher, but the process we see going on is still clearly one of learning with assistance. The talk between the girls reveals that Emily does not seem to have grasped the distinction between *area* and *volume*. Or, to be more precise, she doesn't seem to understand how a mathematical measure of volume (which she is perfectly capable of calculating) relates to the actual capacity of a three-dimensional object. It is interesting to consider how this kind of misunderstanding could arise for a child who (according to her teacher) was good at the computational aspects of mathematics. One possible reason is that school mathematics is so often a book-bound activity, in which few strong connections are made with the world of concrete objects in all their shapes and sizes.[3] It is possible to spend a lot of time calculating areas, volumes, angles, gradients and so on without ever having to consider how these concepts relate to the real world. The sequence thus supports the view that practical, concrete investigations can be valuable for developing mathematical understanding.

But Sequence 2.3 is also useful for illustrating the importance of language in this kind of learning, in three related ways. First, it shows how *argument* can be an important part of the process of learning. And second, how some important kinds of learning are more likely to happen when learners are able to talk and work together without a teacher. It is hard to imagine Emily defending her point of view so vociferously in a conversation with a teacher; much more likely is the possibility that she would keep quiet to hide her confusion. Thirdly, it shows how practical, hands-on activity can gain new depths of meaning if it is talked about. Because it involves a practical task, the maths problem forces Emily to relate her maths to material reality, and so in this sense the physical 'hands-on' experience is very important. But because it is also a joint task, she has the opportunity to solve it by using language as a social mode of thinking. The learning is in the talk, and the talk is about the shared insights of Emily and her partners. On the tape recording, Emily's sudden realisation —'Oh yeh' — is quite apparent. Her understanding is not gained passively from her companions, or through individualised 'discovery learning', but through argumentative talk in which she and her companions explain, contest and justify their views. The talk generated by the activity forces her to revise and extend the contextual framework for her mathematical thinking. Her improved understanding is a joint, social, communicative accomplishment.

I recorded the next sequence at an Open University summer school for teachers which was part of an in-service course on language and literacy. Students spent some of the time at this summer school in study-groups, with about 12 students working on one topic with a tutor. In this particular session, I was the tutor. The session had been set up to bring together students who had expressed an interest in developing new ways of using books in school. The course team had given the session the supposedly bland title of 'Book Choices', and made some suggestions for issues that could be covered in a Summer School booklet for students. The session created unforeseen problems for me as a tutor. Much of this related to the title, 'Book Choices'. When the group first met, it emerged fairly quickly that most of the students felt that they shouldn't be in a session called that. For example:

Sequence 2.4: Book choices

Student A:	Did you put Book Choices down on your form?
Voices in unison:	No!
Student B:	Neither did I.
Student C:	I wanted to do something with literature, not skills.
Student D:	In the stuff they sent us it said you'd be in a group doing one of your choices.
Tutor:	I don't think, I can see what you mean, but I don't think that we need to worry too much about the name. We can always change it. Let's think what we want to do. [*but a little later*]
Student D:	You don't just *choose* books, do you? I *use* them, you know, in different ways.
Student C:	Does it mean buying books? I only have £70 to spend.

Tutor: Look, let's look at what it says in the Summer School booklet: (*reading*) 'the purposes and criteria for selecting...' umm 'responding to children's own choices...'

Sequence 2.4 involves a group of people who were meeting for the first time and who were about to begin a joint learning activity. They did not know each other, but they had spent the last six months studying 'at a distance' the same Open University course. Until that day, Summer School had been something they all knew was going to happen (it was a compulsory element of the course), but about which they had no first-hand experience. One likely influence on their expectations would be the Summer School booklet (sent to them some weeks before). Another would be the form that they completed in advance to express their special interests within the field of language and literacy. In this first study-group session, information and experience already held in *common* were for the first time *shared*. This was achieved by asking about each other's expressed choices and for each other's interpretations of the title of the session. This is often a very important part of the process of learning, especially in formal education — one way to check your own interpretation of ideas and monitor your own progress is to compare your understandings with those of other students. Surprisingly, perhaps, this 'validating' aspect of communication in the classroom has not figured much in the study of teaching and learning.

You can see from Sequence 2.4 that members of the group exerted considerable pressure on me, the tutor, to justify the title and their allocation to the group. In response to this pressure (perfectly legitimate but unusual: most students did not question these things so vociferously), I tried to side-step the problem by suggesting that the group should define its own agenda. Later, I strongly resisted the argument from the students that the whole set of study-groups for the Summer School should be reorganised, as I knew that this would cause administrative chaos. Also, I dreaded the possibility of it emerging that I was the only tutor who had failed to 'manage a group'. I therefore tried to defend and maintain the status quo, as teachers often do, with an appeal to a higher authority as represented in a text (the Summer School booklet).

Amongst other things, Sequence 2.4 is useful for illustrating how power relationships involved in the construction of knowledge can be quite complex. It is certainly the case that someone in the professional role of teacher is in a more powerful position than students because the teacher controls access to the 'right answers' and makes evaluations of students' progress. But this does not give teachers an unassailable position of power and respect in the classroom, merely resources for establishing an authoritative role in their relationship with their students. Despite being 'powerful', teachers may lose control of events. Teachers are also professionally accountable for the management of their learners and for teaching a set curriculum. That is, they are themselves subject to the power of authorities outside the classroom. We have to take all of this into account in analysing what people say and do in the classroom.

Sequence 2.4 also shows, in a fairly mild way, how an assertive group of learners can question and stall the learning activities planned by a teacher. As all experienced teachers know, problems of this kind can be serious because there can be no progress without some acceptance of the legitimacy and the value of activities by both teachers and learners. On this occasion, the fact that my students were themselves professional teachers, and what is more teachers who had given up a week of their holidays to attend Summer School, may have made them particularly critical participants. Of course, every teacher will, at some time, have faced learners who are best described as 'bloody-minded'; I have had far worse challenges to my authority than Sequence 2.4 (unrecorded, unfortunately), and for some teachers serious challenges are a weekly or daily occurrence. The week's events proved that my students did not lack enthusiasm or commitment. What they lacked was a rationale for the activity they were expected to do. Even willing students are unlikely to maintain enthusiasm and commitment if they do not understand the point and purpose of the tasks they are asked to engage in by a teacher. Yet in so many schools and other educational institutions it is assumed that such things can be taken for granted: students are not given any clear indication of why or how they are meant to set about doing things, what exactly they are expected to achieve, or what criteria will be used to evaluate their performance.

We come now to the first sequence that involves a schoolteacher and a class of children. It comes from the beginning of a lesson in a British primary school which was video-recorded when I was working on an Open University course for teachers. The teacher was preparing his whole class of ten- and eleven-year-olds for a series of computer-based activities related to the science curriculum. He told us that the three lessons we would be recording would be about 'keys'. He used this term to mean a binary choice, 'yes–no' system for classifying items according to their distinctive characteristics. At this early stage (this is the second lesson of the series), the children were not working at the computers but doing pencil-and-paper activities on 'keys'. At the point the sequence begins, the whole class are seated on the floor in front of the teacher.

Sequence 2.5: Key questions

Teacher: Good morning folks. Now. We're going to um follow up the work we were doing last week on the keys. Can anyone just remind us: what do we mean by *key*? Colin?

Colin: It's a way of finding out what different things are by using some questions.

Teacher: That's right. Yeh. There was something special about the sort of questions you had to ask, though, wasn't there? What was quite important about the way you asked the questions? Helen?

Helen: You had to separate the two... You had to separate the things into two groups.

Teacher: Yeh. You had to get them into two groups. So *how* would you, how would you word the question? What type of question would you have to have? Helen?

Helen: Yes or no.

Teacher: Yes. We had to have a 'yes or no' answer. So you would say something... If it was the class, let's say, how might you divide this group into two? Philip?

Philip: Girls and boys.

Teacher: Girls and boys. So what would be the question you'd ask?

Philip: Er, are you a boy?

Teacher: Are you a boy. Then you'd say 'yes' in your case or 'no' in Heather's case. Right, good. Now that's the basic principle. And how can we go further, say with the class?
Let's say we've already divided into boys and girls. What's another question you can now ask to divide those two groups? (*pausa*) Katie?

Katie: Have they got dark hair?

Teacher: Have they got dark hair? And is that a good question for both groups? Remember, we've got boys and girls. Remember, we've got boys and girls? (*Unintelligible mumble from pupils*)

Teacher: It's a question that applies to both groups that, so it's a good question. That's right.
What would be a *bad* question to ask there, which wouldn't fit in with the key? Graham?

Graham: Have you got long hair?

Teacher: Have you got long hair? Why wouldn't that be a good question?

Graham: Because girls might have long hair but boys wouldn't.

Teacher: Right. Certainly now. Nowadays. Might have been a good
                 question 20 years ago.[4]

In this sequence we can see the teacher first of all attempting to establish
some continuity between last week's work and the task in hand. He checks
the children's understanding of the central concept of 'key' by *eliciting* from
some of them what he sees as its crucial features and providing feedback
on their answers. He uses the contributions of those who remember what
they have done to remind others who may not. He could have simply
reminded them himself, but by using this technique he is able to both check
the recall of some learners and also present the knowledge as something
which is now owned by the children as well as himself. He takes up the
examples they offer in their responses and uses them to carry the discussion
in the direction he thinks it needs to go. The whole sequence is a
conversational routine which can only happen if everyone who participates
knows the rules for 'doing lessons', the conventional ways for talking like
a teacher or a pupil. At another level it is a particular and peculiar kind of
problem-solving task. The children are asked how they might use questions
to divide the class into girls and boys. This requires a 'willing suspension
of disbelief', a temporary detachment from the real world on the part of all
concerned, for it is obvious that no interrogative procedures would really
be required to tell the boys and girls apart. This kind of problem-solving
also has its own rules, which those who have gone through school usually
come to take for granted. Research has shown that 'unschooled' adults are
often unfamiliar with such procedures and resistant to such deliberate
misrepresentations of real-world circumstances.[5]

In one remark — 'that's the basic principle' — the teacher points to what
the children are really meant to have learnt the previous week, and what
they are concerned with now. They are learning how to construct a
classification system based on binary choices. The procedures they follow
are meant to give them practice in doing this; which particular set of objects
they go on to classify is, at this point, of no special educational significance.
It is crucial for the learning and the educational progress of these children
that they recognise that a principle is being taught, and do not focus their
attention on more obvious but relatively trivial features of the task.
Whether they do so or not will very much depend on how well the teacher
helps them to see the wood for the trees, the principle behind the
procedures.

Classroom question-and-answer routines like Sequence 2.5 can be used
as one very effective strategy for guiding the construction of knowledge.
But while there are good reasons for teachers to use such routines, there are

also some good reasons for using them sparingly and only as part of a wider repertoire of communicative activities. For one thing, the opportunities for learners to make any kind of active contribution is severely limited. All they can do is provide responses in the 'slots' provided, so the course of events is determined more by the teacher's understanding of the topic than by the gaps in students' understanding of it. And while the 'right answers' of some pupils may be informative for the rest of the class, in routines like this the number of pupils who are able to contribute is only a tiny proportion of the whole. What is more, any teacher who does want the answers to be models for the rest of the class is likely to direct his or her questions to the most able, confident and articulate pupils, thus excluding and possibly demoralising others. Learners need to get involved with new knowledge in order to consolidate their own understanding, and this cannot be done just through hearing information being presented clearly and logically by an expert. They will almost certainly need to try to use it themselves, under different conditions, if they are to make the knowledge their own.

There is no good reason why the teacher should make a once-and-for-all choice between using 'traditional', whole-class, didactic methods or the more open-ended discussions and group activities associated with 'progressive' or 'child-centred' education. The problem is how to provide learners with the right balance of different kinds of opportunities and guidance. In fact, the teacher in Sequence 2.5 went on to organise his pupils into pairs and small groups, and he guided their learning in quite different ways on those occasions. The supposed choice between 'progressive', 'child-centred' methods and formal, traditional methods of instruction is a dilemma which a socio-cultural perspective on teaching and learning helps us to side-step. I will return to these matters later in the book (especially in Chapters 5 and 6).

Summary and Conclusions

Despite some obvious differences in style and content, the conversational sequences I have included in this chapter have some important things in common. In all of them people appear to establish some shared understanding. In all of them, someone asserts some intellectual authority during the event. And all of them represent the joint pursuit of some kind of learning. They all show language being used as a tool, a social mode of thinking, for the development of knowledge and understanding. In events like those I have illustrated, knowledge is neither accumulated nor discovered by learners: it is shaped by people's communicative actions.

Different kinds of conversational activities offer different ways of engaging with knowledge and developing understanding.

I also showed that the process of constructing knowledge is one in which power and influence are inevitably exerted, and sometimes contested. Of course, the use of talk to exert power and influence over the construction of knowledge is not peculiar to classrooms, or to the process of teaching and learning. In law, science, politics, business, life at home and in the street, particular versions of knowledge, of 'the truth', emerge because someone is able, in some way and on some particular occasion, to convince others of the validity — or at least the social value — of their version. Schools and other educational institutions are special, however, because their explicit purpose is teaching and learning, because power and responsibility are formally vested in the teacher, and because teachers are usually expected to teach a set curriculum, a given body of knowledge. Any analysis of how teachers use language should take full account of these factors. In the next chapter, I will look at some of the strategies that teachers use to represent and emphasise what they think needs to be learned.

Notes

1. Rogoff, B. (1990) *Apprenticeship in Thinking:* New York: Oxford University Press.
2. Sequence 2.3 is included as Band 2 on the audiocassette for the Open University INSET pack *Talk and Learning 5–16* (Open University, 1991a). The recording was provided by the Croydon Oracy Project.
3. See Nunes, T. *et al.* (1993) *Street Mathematics and School Mathematics.* Cambridge: Cambridge University Press.
4. Sequence 2.4 comes from a video recording for the Open University course EH232 *Computers and Learning.* Milton Keynes: The Open University (1991b).
5. See, for example, the conversations with Kpelle people of Liberia reported by Michael Cole and Sylvia Scribner (1974) in *Culture and Thought.* New York: Wiley. See also Cole, M. and Means, B. (1981) *Comparative Studies of How People Think: An Introduction.* Cambridge, MA: Harvard University Press.

3 Guidance Strategies

In the last chapter, I provided some illustrations of how learning can be guided through different kinds of conversation. Looking across societies, or even into the lives of different social groups within the same society, we can find some interesting differences and preferences in styles for how talk is used to guide the construction of knowledge. Reviewing a wide field of research, Barbara Rogoff[1] describes a wonderful variety in the ways that mothers habitually interact with young children. In some cultures, for example, eye contact with infants seems to be almost completely avoided, while in others it is actively sought. In some communities adults do a lot of telling and explaining to young children, but elsewhere we find that children are rarely offered verbal explanations about how to do things and instead are expected to learn from example or inference. In all these societies, most children grow up knowledgeable and competent in the life of their community. It is also fascinating to find that what members of one community consider a commonsensical strategy for encouraging children's development may seem nonsensical to people in other communities with different habits. For example, Shirley Brice Heath quotes the following comments by a grandmother from one black working-class community in the southeastern USA about the strange practice she has observed among white people of quizzing children about their knowledge:

> White folks uh hear dey kids say sump'n, dey say it back to 'em, dey aks 'em 'gain 'n 'gain 'bout things, like they 'posed to be born knowin'. You think I kin tell Teegie [her grandson] all he gotta know to get along? He just gotta be keen, keep his eyes open, don't he be sorry. [2]

Most research on the guidance of learning has focused on parents and very young children at home, but here I want to concentrate on teaching and learning in schools and other educational institutions. In most countries of the world, formal schooling has now been introduced for at least some of the population. Many developing education systems show the heavy influence of western European conceptions of how schoolchildren should be taught, and this process of development has almost inevitably been at the expense of pre-existing, traditional forms of

education. But while western educational influences are apparent world-
wide, some educationalists and researchers have recently argued for a
reconsideration of the value of other traditional methods of guidance for
teaching in schools. Describing traditional methods of education which
were common in rural communities in Zimbabwe, Amos Munjanja[3]
comments on the importance of 'education by recitation' — a mode which,
although perhaps continued in some informal language games like the
'paired counting' illustrated in Sequence 2.2 in Chapter 2, has fallen out of
favour in the homes and schools of most European communities. Through
a language recitation game called *Dudu muduri*, a child in a Zimbabwean
Shona village would learn the names of all the local families. At another
time, children would come together and play a game in which the players
named all the trees. Munjanja remarks 'the sharing of knowledge in groups
that we may call 'classes' was carried out while people were gathered
together for entertainment...story-telling...worship...doing some work...
[or] an important event such as a funeral'. In these ways, education was
kept a part of everyday life, rather than a separate, institutionalized activity.
He suggests that Zimbabwean schoolteachers should look for occasions
when they can step out of their normally unemotional, detached role and
interact more with learners in the non-authoritarian manner of the 'aunt'
or 'uncle' in tribal communities.

A reappraisal of non-European educational traditions is also encouraged
by research by the anthropologist Ruth Paradise[4] in native American
communities in Mexico. To western eyes, native American adults seem to
make little conscious effort to support or guide the learning of their
children, compared with the more interactive and interventional style
which is the norm in European and American middle-class cultures. Earlier
research (for example by Susan Philips[5]) had focused on the problems
which this kind of learning experience created for native American children
when they entered schools (which were inevitably based on more active,
interventional styles of teaching). However, from her observations in
Mazahua communities in Mexico, Paradise suggests that the more passive
involvement of adults can encourage children to take a more active role in
the management of their own learning, producing 'children who are able
to take responsibility for their own learning, who are able to create
situations and activities from which to learn, children with a highly
developed capacity for taking initiative and sustaining personal motiva-
tion'.[4]

I am sure that there is no point in comparing, in absolute terms, the
effectiveness of different ways of guiding the construction of knowledge.
Different kinds of teaching may be best for helping different kinds of

learning and the development of different kinds of understanding.[6] Teaching-and-learning also has to be carried out in ways which take account of the setting and the relationships involved. One teacher with a class cannot provide the same opportunities for sustained supportive interaction as a mother at home with an infant. On the other hand, classrooms offer opportunities for joint learning which an isolated child might be denied. So we must evaluate guidance strategies in context. But in any given set of circumstances there is bound to be a range of possible options for how guidance is provided.

To return to non-European traditions, G.D. Jayalakshmi[7] suggests that in secondary education in India one can see the continuing influence of the traditional *Gurukala* and *Harikatha* styles of instruction and storytelling, which depended upon the performance of an effective storyteller (the teacher) and a receptive audience (the pupils). In *Gurukala* the guru would typically sit on a raised platform and talk to students seated in rows. The guru would explain texts to the students, who did most of their learning by rote. This method was intended to provide students with access to knowledge which resided, unequivocally, in the authority of the teacher and of the text (*Harikatha* literally means 'the tale of the gods'.) Describing life in a modern secondary school in Bhojpur, Jayalakshmi says 'Although the students...did not have to memorise their lessons, the education system seems to be similar — it implicitly recognizes the teacher's superior knowledge and points to his importance, centrality and authority. He is seen as a repository of knowledge and his task is to transmit this to his less knowledgeable students'.[8] These traditional methods have served Indian scholars well for generations and, as Jayalakshmi also points out, they have been combined with British influences to generate a distinct and well-established Indian style of classroom communication. Amongst other features, this style involves the frequent use of rhetorical questions by the teacher, marked by intonation, pauses or gestures, which the students are not expected to answer. Such questions are marked by the symbol (?) in the following example. In it, a teacher in Bhojpur is telling his students the story of how the Reuter international news agency arose from Paul Reuter's search for an exciting and rewarding profession:

Teacher: A bookseller is here and, a circus lady is there. A girl or a boy working in circus. Who is having excitement in his profession?

Teacher and students: A circus girl.

Teacher: Or a circus boy. Once I was watching just a circus. And I simultaneously started making a poem. Because I was seeing

(?) an exciting profession. In bookselling there is no excitement, OK? Just reading and taking books. There is no excitement. There is no excitement in taking a food which is without salt. But there is excitement in taking what (?) chicken. Well spiced, nicely spiced. Understand? So, people should have excitement in their profession. There are people who wish, who crave for excitement in their profession. And this very excitement is what (?) a life force, force of life, that, and that is an energy, a wonderful energy that scientists may well research about. So Reuter didn't find excitement in bookselling. (*reads*) And he sold off his bookselling...[9]

However, Jayalakshmi also recorded the way that this well-established, teacher-dominated pattern of interaction broke down with the introduction of a video-led instruction 'package' for teaching English, which involved students in active collaboration in small groups in the classroom. It seemed that the introduction of a new, authoritative source of information and of new patterns of communication undermined teachers' control of the discourse. In this new setting, the traditional guidance strategies were just not viable. Talk amongst students began to occur even while a teacher was still speaking. Teachers varied in the extent to which they were able to cope with these changes, with some becoming uncertain and dispirited.

We can see, then, that while a range of ways for guiding the construction of knowledge exists, the patterns of communication in any classroom are not defined simply by the teacher's personal style of teaching. In any school or other educational institution, the ways that teachers and learners talk will be shaped by cultural traditions and by the specific institutional settings in which they operate. The great majority of teachers take these established ways for granted, whatever they are. But while teachers have to live with some constraints of working in schools, they do not need to be the slaves of convention. They can become critically aware of the ways they use language, whether these are a matter of cultural convention or personal style. A question which teachers and researchers need to address is whether established, habitual ways of talking provide, in the circumstances, the best kinds of guidance.

Classroom research suggests that there is often a mis-match between how things are taught and how and what students are expected to learn. To return to India, this is well illustrated by research by Urvashi Sahni[10] on how literacy was taught in rural primary schools in one Indian locality. She found that the style of the teachers' talk to their classes was harshly authoritarian and that children's contributions were rarely encouraged and commonly suppressed. Opportunities for children's active, purposeful use of the written language were also extremely limited. Sahni suggests that the oppressive communicative relationship between the teachers and pupils reflected the power relationships in the local education system as a whole, within which teachers were themselves rigidly managed and cowed by their superiors. She points out that classroom ways of using spoken and written language were totally at odds with the stated aims of the government education initiative supposedly being pursued at the time, which was intended to increase the 'personal empowerment' of students through literacy.

In the next section, I want to look at some of the particular ways that teachers talk (which I have called 'techniques') when they are trying to guide the construction of knowledge by their students. Although I will describe each technique in general terms, I am not suggesting that any of them are, in themselves, 'good' or 'bad' techniques for guiding the construction of knowledge. They cannot be evaluated out of context or without taking into account what is being talked about. Classroom conversations have histories and futures and they involve people who have relationships and cultural backgrounds; ways of speaking that work for some teachers and learners would not work for others. If we ignore content and context, we miss the nature of language as a social mode of thinking. But if we accept their significance, we can then begin to understand and evaluate events in real classrooms.

Some Techniques used by Teachers

Teachers in schools and other educational institutions use language to pursue their professional aims and goals. One of their aims is to guide the learning activity of their students along directions required by a curriculum, and to try to construct a joint, shared version of educational knowledge with their students. There are certain common techniques that teachers use to try to achieve this. Teachers may not necessarily be self-consciously aware of the techniques they use; and teachers will vary as to how much and how well they use any of them. But these techniques are intentional, goal-directed ways of talking nevertheless, which reflect the constraints of the institutional setting in which schoolteachers work. In attempting to guide learning, they use talk to do three things:

(a) *elicit relevant knowledge from students*, so that they can see what students already know and understand and so that the knowledge is seen to be 'owned' by students as well as teachers;

(b) *respond to things that students say*, not only so that students get feedback on their attempts but also so that the teacher can incorporate what students say into the flow of the discourse and gather students' contributions together to construct more generalized meanings.

(c) *describe the classroom experiences that they share with students* in such a way that the educational significance of those joint experiences is revealed and emphasised.

I will discuss each of these in turn.

(a) Eliciting Knowledge From Students

For obvious reasons, teachers ask for information that students know but the teacher does not — about how well they are progressing in activities, about their rationale for doing things in certain ways, and even (occasionally) about their experiences outside school. But teachers also often ask questions to which they already know the answers, because they need to know if the students know those answers too. If they ask such a question of a class or group and one member is unable to provide the required answer, a teacher will typically ask another student, and perhaps then another if a 'right' answer is still not forthcoming. If no-one seems able to answer, we might expect that a teacher would simply tell the class the answer. But providing the answer is one thing that it seems that teachers are often at great pains to avoid. Instead, they may resort to what Derek Edwards and I called *cued elicitation*,[11] which is a way of drawing out from students the information they are seeking — the 'right' answers to their questions — by providing strong visual clues and verbal hints as to what answer is required. Here is one of the examples we observed, in a primary school lesson about pendulums. Cued elicitation may be achieved just by wording a question in a certain way, but often, as in this example, other features of the talk are important. I have therefore shown words that the teacher said emphatically in bold type, and described non-verbal activity in the right-hand column. The teacher began by describing Galileo sitting in church, 'very bored', when his attention was taken by an incense burner swinging above...

Sequence 3.1: Galileo's pulse

Teacher:...and he wanted to time it, just for interest's sake, just to see how long it took to make a complete swing. Now he didn't have a watch, but he had on him something that was a very good timekeeper that he could use to hand straight away.

Teacher begins to swing her hand back and forward in rhythm, as she talks.

Teacher snaps her fingers on 'straight

	away' and looks invitingly at pupils as if posing a question or inviting a response.
You've got it. I've got it. What is it? What could we use to count beats? What have **you** got?	*Teacher points on 'You've' and 'I've'. She beats her hand on the table slowly, looking around the group of pupils who smile and shrug.*
You can feel it **here**.	*Teacher puts her fingers on her wrist.*
Pupils: Pulse.	*Speaking in near unison.*
Teacher: A pulse. Everybody see if you can find it.	*All copy her, feeling their wrists.*

Cued elicitation is particularly popular with teachers who are trying to teach a curriculum in 'progressive', 'learner-centred ways', but the use of this particular teaching technique is widespread and long-established (it can be seen in the Socratic dialogues constructed by Plato).[12] Why do teachers use this technique? One likely reason is so that learners have to take an active part, however small, in the dialogue. The teacher avoids continuous monologue or the mere provision of missing information. Another possible reason is that the cueing procedure may act as a mnemonic or *aide-mémoire*, a small memorable event which helps learners remember. Teachers sometimes create formulaic phrases for this same purpose (so on another occasion this teacher encouraged the children to remember that, for pendulums, the rule was 'the shorter the string, the faster the swing'). It is also worth noting here that the teacher in Sequence 3.1 is *storytelling*: she introduces children to information about Galileo's discoveries through a narrative style that is very similar to the Indian teacher's account of the origins of Reuters on page 24. It is perhaps too often forgotten in the analysis of teaching and learning, that one legitimate goal for a teacher is to make information *memorable*. Think back through your own experience: is any of the academic information you recall embedded in a narrative? (The story of Darwin's voyage through the south seas on the Beagle was an explicit and important part of my biology education at school. Chemistry, in contrast, seemed to lack such voyages of discovery and I remember much less of it.) Narratives — interesting ones — can provide effective ways of *formulating* knowledge so that students can reconstruct it later.[13]

The trouble with questions

One way that the teacher in Sequence 3.1 achieved her cued elicitation was through asking some questions. There has been a lot of research on the kinds and number of questions teachers ask. We know from such research that teachers do typically ask a great many questions, but that, if British primary teachers are typical, the majority of those questions are concerned with managing the class. (Examples might be 'Alison, have you got your book?' 'Yes Miss'; or the more rhetorical: 'Terry, what did I tell you before?' 'To stay at my own desk Miss'.) Reporting the findings of the Leverhulme Primary Project, George Brown and Ted Wragg[14] comment that of 1021 recorded questions spoken by primary teachers, 57% could be classified as 'managerial'. We also know that teachers tolerate very short silences after asking a question, and that by leaving longer pauses they could encourage a much higher rate of response from their students.

There is some controversy in educational research about the use of questions as a strategy for guiding the construction of knowledge.[15] For example, David Wood argues that teachers' questions often constrain and limit the directions of classroom discussion in quite unfortunate ways. By requiring short, factual answers, he suggests, teachers may actually inhibit pupils' intellectual activity. Reviewing research on the teaching of children of various ages, he concludes that 'The extent to which a child reveals his or her own ideas and seeks information is inversely proportioned to the frequency of teacher questions'.[16] Taking part in a series of formal question-and-answer sessions only offers opportunities for some limited kinds of learning. What is more, teachers' insistence on 'correct answers' may confuse students about the main focus of their learning — is it what they know or how they say it that is important? That is, students may be more worried about 'doing the right thing' than with thinking things through. This is an important point, and one that is well illustrated by some research done by Jo Arthur[17] in classrooms in Botswana. The teachers she observed were teaching mathematics, but they also used question-and-answer sessions as opportunities for schooling children in the use of formal English. For example, she found that primary teachers commonly insisted that pupils reply to questions 'in full sentences', as in this example from a maths lesson:

Teacher: How many parts are left here [First pupil's name]?
First pupil: Seven parts.
Teacher: Answer fully. How many parts are there?
Pupil: There are...there are seven parts.
Teacher: How many parts are left? Sit down my boy. You have tried. Yes [second pupil's name] ?
Second pupil: We are left with seven parts.

Teacher: We are left with seven parts. Say that [second pupil's name].

Second pupil: We are left with seven parts.

Teacher: Good boy. We are left with seven parts.[18]

This sequence is made up of variants of the kind of classic teacher–pupil exchanges recorded by language researchers the world over, and usually called an IRF or IRE because they consist of three parts: an *Initiation* by the teacher; a *Response* by the pupils; and some *Feedback* (or *Evaluation*) by the teacher to that response.[19] For example:

How many parts are left here? [Initiation] Seven parts [Response] Answer fully [Feedback/Evaluation]

The teacher was using these exchanges not only to evaluate the mathematical understanding of the students, but also to enforce one of the 'ground rules' for classroom talk ('speak in full sentences') that she operated in her classroom.

David Wood's own research shows that when teachers use other kinds of conversational strategies, such as offering their own reflective observations, this can encourage pupils to do likewise and can generate longer and more animated responses from pupils. He provides a good example of a nursery teacher using these other techniques and getting animated and extended responses from two four-year-old children.[20] But this brings me back to the need to evaluate any strategies for guidance in terms of the particular circumstances in which they are used, and to take account of the kind of knowledge involved. Nursery teachers are usually not working to the imperative of a set curriculum; and even those who have a given curriculum are never so precisely accountable as are teachers in primary and secondary schools (especially those in Britain since the introduction of a National Curriculum in 1988). The goals of nursery teaching normally include encouraging children to practise and extend the use of their mother tongue. But the amount of lively talk which goes on during teaching-and-learning is not, in itself, a measure of the quality of the process. For most teachers in schools, the crucial issue is maintaining a suitable balance between, on the one hand, offering children opportunities for open-ended exploration and discussion and, on the other, fulfilling a responsibility for achieving established curriculum goals. It is generally accepted that this is a difficult balance to achieve.

If I am less convinced than some researchers by the evidence against the use of questions as a teaching technique, this is partly because I am sceptical of the value of studying 'questions' as such. If one is interested in what teachers actually say and do with language, the value of categorizing and quantifying 'questions' is limited. Unfortunately for language researchers, people do not reliably use the same grammatical forms of speech to pursue the same purposes. As Douglas Barnes and Frankie Todd put it, 'speaker-hearers choose freely from a number of devices which carry out varied functions, and they use these forms in an innovative and varied fashion. Forms are shaped to the purpose of speakers, and not vice-versa'.[21] If you again read Sequence 3.1, you will see that the teacher achieves a 'cued elicitation' not only by using questions, but through a combination of various verbal and non-verbal strategies. Also, as I mentioned earlier, any analysis or evaluation of talk must take account of the fact that all conversations have a history and a future and take place between particular people in a specific place and time. Direct questioning might sometimes be appropriate, and at other times not. Talk is always 'situated'. This might be hard for analysts to deal with; but, frankly, we have no choice.

There are some interesting examples of a secondary school teacher using questions to good effect in Sequence 3.2 (below), which was video-recorded in a school in Derbyshire. As part of their English studies, a class of fourteen-year-olds were engaged in an extended computer-based communication with children in a nearby primary school. In a 'fantasy adventure' setting, the secondary students were (in groups of three) pretending to be a group of characters stranded in time and space. Explanations of their predicaments and requests for solutions were e-mailed to the primary children, whose responses were considered and used by each group of students to develop the story further. Sequence 3.2 is one small part of a recorded session in which their English teacher was questioning one group of girls about the most recent interaction and their future plans.

Sequence 3.2: Dimensions

Teacher: What about the word 'dimension', because you were going to include that in your message, weren't you?

Anne: Yeh. And there's going to be — if they go in the right room, then they'll find a letter in the floor and that'll spell 'dimension'.

Teacher: What happens if they do go in the wrong room?

Emma: Well, there's no letter in the bottom, in the floor.

Teacher: Oh God! So they've got to get it right, or that's it! (*everyone laughs*) The adventurers are stuck there for ever. And Cath can't get back to her own time. What do you mean the letters are in the room, I don't quite follow that?

Emma: On the floor, like a tile or something.

Teacher:	Oh I see. Why did you choose the word 'dimension'?
Anne:	Don't know (*the three pupils speak together, looking to each other, seeming uncertain*)
Emma:	It just came up. Just said, you know, 'dimension' and everyone agreed.
Sharon:	Don't know.
Teacher:	Right, because it seemed to fit in with, what, the fantasy flow, flavour?
Sharon:	Yeh.
Teacher:	OK. Why do they go through the maze rather than go back? I mean what motivation do they have for going through it in the first place?
Emma:	Um, I think that it was the king told them that Joe would be in the maze or at the end of the maze, and they didn't go back because of Joe, think it was. I'm not sure about that.
Teacher:	You've really got to sort that out. It's got to be very, very clear.[22]

In Sequence 3.2 the teacher uses questions to draw out from the students the content of their recent e-mail message, and also some justifications for what they included in it. In some ways, her language is classic 'teacher-talk'. Most of her questions are ones to which she does *not* already know the answer; but she certainly evaluates the answers she receives. There are the recognizable *Initiation–Response–Feedback* (IRF) exchanges (such as the last exchange in the sequence). At one level, she is simply monitoring their activity and assessing the adequacy of their attempt to continue the communication with the younger children. But her questions are not just assessment, they are *part of her teaching*. Like many effective teachers, she is using her enquiries not only to monitor children's activity, but also to guide it. Through questions like 'Why did you choose the word "dimension"?' and 'Why do they go through the maze rather than go back?' she directs their attention to matters requiring more thought and clarification. In fact, it is only when the questions she asks are considered in context, as one element of her whole interaction with the pupils, that we can see how she uses language to guide her students' endeavours.

The same kind of question, or even the same words, can be used by teachers to very different effect on different occasions. In an analysis, at the very least, we need to look at who is speaking to whom, and what else has been said and done by those people. If we want to evaluate the use of questions as techniques for guiding the construction of knowledge, there is no alternative. Of course, it may well be the case that many teachers employ a repertoire of techniques for eliciting knowledge which is unnecessarily narrow. In the interests of healthy innovation, Tony Edwards has suggested that teachers might usefully consider some of the following techniques when they are trying to initiate or extend discussions. They might try:

- making a declarative (open-ended or provocative) statement which invites a rejoinder or disagreement;
- inviting elaboration ('Could you say a bit more about that?');
- admitting perplexity when it occurs, whether about the topic itself or about a pupil's contribution to it;
- encouraging questions from pupils (rare in many classrooms);
- maintaining silence at strategic points (Dillon [another classroom researcher][23] suggests that three to five seconds may be enough to draw in another pupil's contribution or encourage the previous speaker to elaborate on what was said).[24]

These seem to be very reasonable suggestions for how teachers might increase the repertoire of techniques that they normally employ. But advocating them begs the question of exactly what, on any particular occasion, a teacher wants and expects to achieve through using them. (The notion of 'maintaining silence at strategic points' implies a *strategy* being used to achieve a goal.) Alternatives to traditional questions may, or may not, provide better teaching in any given situation; it all depends on the judgement of the teacher in that context.

(b) Responding to What Students Say

As illustrated by Sequence 3.2 above, one of the ways that teachers sustain dialogues with their students is to use what students say as the basis for what they say next. In this way, the learners' own remarks are incorporated into the teaching–learning process. The most obvious way of doing this is through *confirmation* (as, for example, a teacher's 'Yes, that's right' to a pupil's answer). *Repetitions* of things learners say are another, which allow the teacher to draw to the attention of a whole class an answer or other remark which is judged by the teacher to have educational significance (look, for example, at how Jo Arthur's Botswana teacher does this on page 28).

Teachers often paraphrase or *reformulate* a pupil's remark, so as to offer the class a revised, tidied-up version of what was said which fits in better with the point that the teacher wishes to make. For example:

Teacher: Right. Heather. What more can you do with a database?
Heather: You can put it…you can sort all the numbers and things.
Teacher: So you can sort out the information as well.

There are also *elaborations*, when a teacher picks up on a cryptic statement made by a pupil and expands and/or explains its significance to the rest of the class. For example, in this extract from Sequence 3.2, the teacher elaborates the student's explanations for the benefit of the whole class:

Teacher: What happens if they do go in the wrong room?
Emma: Well, there's no letter in the bottom, in the floor.
Teacher: Oh God! So they've got to get it right, or that's it! (*everyone laughs*) The adventurers are stuck there for ever. And Cath can't get back to her own time.

Wrong answers or unsuitable contributions may be explicitly *rejected* by a teacher. But we should also note a popular technique that teachers have for dealing with wrong answers — simply ignoring them.

(c) Describing Shared Classroom Experience

An important task for a teacher is to help students see how the various activities they do, over time, contribute to the development of their understanding. Education cannot be merely the experience of a series of consecutive events, it must be a developmental process in which earlier experiences provide the foundations for making sense of later ones. For those involved in teaching and learning, continuity of shared experience is one of the most precious resources available. There are many ways that teachers try to create continuities in the experience of learners — by sequencing activities in certain ways, by dealing with topics in order of difficulty, and so on. I am concerned here with how they help learners perceive continuity in what they are doing. Through language there is the possibility of repeatedly revisiting and reinterpreting that experience, and of using it as the basis for future talk, activity and learning.

'*We*' *statements* (as in a teacher saying to a class 'last week we learned how to measure angles') are often used when teachers are trying to represent past experience as relevant to present activity. They show how teachers help learners see that they have significant past experience in common, and so have gained shared knowledge and collective understanding which can be drawn upon to progress further. Teachers also often *recap* for the benefit of the class what has gone in earlier in a lesson, and in previous lessons. An interesting variant of this is when they *reconstructively recap* what has been said and done by themselves and the children on earlier occasions, 'rewriting history' so as to make events fit better into their pedagogic framework. While this can be useful for helping learners see the wood for the trees, it may create problems if the 'reconstruction' is too imaginative to fit the events as remembered by the learners themselves. (As

Table 1: Some techniques that teachers use...

...to elicit knowledge from learners

  Direct elicitations

  Cued elicitations

...to respond to what learners say

  Confirmations

  Rejections

  Repetitions

  Elaborations

  Reformulations

...to describe significant aspects of shared experience

  'We' statements

  Literal recaps

  Reconstructive recaps

---

when a science teacher referred to the lesson in which 'we made a vacuum', when nearly all of the students' attempts had failed!)

The various techniques which I have described being used by teachers to construct joint, shared versions of educational knowledge with their students are listed in Table 1.

The techniques listed in Table 1 are also found in the talk of teachers who work in places other than schools, as the next sequence shows. It is one of several sessions that my colleagues and I recorded of teaching and learning within a British occupational training programme for young people aged 16–18. This session was one of a series on work-related literacy, in which a tutor followed up aspects of literacy that the trainees encountered in their work placements. On this occasion, the main topic was 'health and safety regulations in the workplace'. Although the tutor had taught all of them before, this was the first time that the five trainees had met as a group. The sequence begins a short time into this first session, as they are sitting round a table with the tutor.

Sequence 3.3: Safety in the home

Tutor:　　　　(*Looking round the group*) Before we start, can anyone give me

	any ideas of the kinds of accidents that might happen in the home?
Kay:	Leaving toys on the stairs.
Tutor:	That's good. Anyone else?
Steve:	Trailing wires such as on an iron…
Tutor:	Fine.
Steve:	…where a little child could pull it down.
Tutor:	Pull it down. Yes, fine. Can you think of anything, Amanda?
Amanda:	Just leaving things hanging around and everywhere, putting pots away…
Tutor:	Mmm. (*nods*)
Amanda:	…and things like that.
Tutor:	So being tidy is one of the main areas. I agree with you (*Amanda nodding head, says 'yeh' while tutor is speaking*).[25]

We can see here the tutor eliciting ideas from the trainees and providing some evaluative comment through *confirmation* ('That's good'), *repetition* ('pull it down') and through making a statement which is both a *reformulation* and a summary *recap* of the discussion ('So being tidy is one of the main areas'). With this final, general statement she gathers into one teaching point the various suggestions made. This 'gathering' together is something people rarely do in 'everyday' conversations. The tutor certainly controls the flow of the discourse, and is the sole evaluator of its content. But (as she explained when I spoke to her afterwards) she is also allowing the individuals to express themselves on the common, everyday topic of experience in the home, and reassuring them of the value of their ideas before she moves into the more difficult language and procedures of work-based safety regulations. In this way, she is trying to set up a small cohesive, supportive community whose knowledge and understanding can be guided by her over the coming weeks.

A common problem for learners entering any new field of knowledge is dealing with new technical terms. Research has provided a wealth of examples of students having problems with these 'difficult words'.[26] One way that teachers can help learners make sense of technical terms is by introducing them into dialogues with pupils in situations where the context helps make meanings clear. The following sequence (recorded in the same classroom as Sequence 3.1, during the research described in *Common Knowledge*) shows how one teacher introduced technical terms (shown in bold type) during an activity on pendulums with a group of four 9- and 10-year-olds. As you read it, notice the terms that the teacher introduces, and her use of 'repetitions' and 'elaborations'.

Sequence 3.4: What is a pendulum?

Teacher: Yes. Let's have a closer look at this one. Right. Now then. What does a pendulum have to have to be a pendulum?
          (*Teacher takes off the pendant she is wearing and puts it on the table*)

Anthony: String.

Teacher: A string, yes. In this case it's a...?
          (*She holds up the pendant's chain*)

Children: Chain.

Teacher: Chain. So it has to be **suspended** doesn't it?
          (*She raises and suspends the pendant by its chain*)

Anthony: A weight.

Teacher: It has to have a weight, doesn't it. A **mass** at the end which this one has.
          [*the discussion continues*]

Karen: It has to hang straight down.

Teacher: It has to hang straight down Karen.
          There it is. So that's right isn't it? So it has to hang from a **fixed point.** It has to be **suspended** from a string or a chain or whatever and it has to have a **mass** at the end. Right.
          (*She holds the pendant so that it hangs vertically*)
          [*Towards the end of the same lesson the teacher checks that the children are able to use these terms themselves*]

Teacher: Now what did we say that they had to have?

Jonathan: A pendulum?

Jonathan: A weight at the bottom.

Teacher: Yes and yours has, OK? And yours is a washer.

Jonathan: Mm.

Teacher: Right. David what else does a pendulum have to have?

David: A **mass**.

Teacher: Jonathan's mentioned that.

David: A string.

Teacher: A string or a chain or some means of hanging it down.
          Right. And Anthony what was the third thing it had to have?

Anthony: **Suspended.**

Teacher: Right. From?

Anthony: **A fixed point.**

We can see that at least some of the children have grasped the new terminology of 'fixed point', 'suspended' and 'mass', and have begun to use it. It is not clear that they fully understood what it all means. (For example, David may not realize that 'mass' means something equivalent to 'weight' here: we were told by the teacher that she planned to explicitly discuss the meanings of these and other relevant terms in a forthcoming lesson.)

In the next sequence, the topic is also science. It comes from a class in a secondary school who have been working with the teacher over a couple of terms.

Sequence 3.5: Preparations for the experiment

Teacher: Right, so we've just read through the actual — Gary — just read through the actual instructions for the experiment. We want to talk a little about the equipment now that we're going to be using a fireproof mat. Um. Debbie, what about the fireproof mat, why's that important? Put it on the table, don't we, why?

Debbie: 'Cos it might burn the table.

Teacher: Yes. Because something in our experiment might burn the table, OK. So we need to have a fireproof mat. It is made of asbestos which doesn't burn in actual fact, which is quite, you know, useful to use. We're going to be using a tripod as well. Sarah, why do we use the tripod? Hannah?

Hannah: To fit the, er, so you can fit the um, the bunsen underneath and have something for things to actually rest on.

Teacher: To actually stand on, OK...What do you need to do to a bunsen when you are not using it?

John: Turn it to a yellow flame.

Teacher: Need to turn it to the yellow flame. Why it that important, Oliver?

Oliver: So that nobody'll put their arms through it.

Teacher: So that nobody'll put their arms through it, OK.[27]

Here we have a classic example of a teacher eliciting from learners a certain special kind of knowledge — things that she knows perfectly well but that she is not sure that they have grasped. She also uses 'we statements' to mark recent past experience as joint ('we've just read through...'), repeating, reformulating and elaborating pupils' contributions (so that 'cos it might burn the table' becomes 'Because something in our experiment might burn the table'). She even goes so far as to represent her aims and intentions as those of the class ('We want to talk a little'...'we need to have...'). The teacher's concerns here seem to be those of safety and the standardization of experimental procedure: the kind of knowledge she is dealing with is to do with *procedures* rather than *principles*, but that need not mean it is not valuable in its own way.[28]

However, this sequence does illustrate how the 'classic' format of teacher–pupil interactions, the I–R–F exchange, can be used by teachers to narrowly constrain the contributions of pupils. It is worth comparing this sequence with the previous two. Unlike Sequence 3.3, the teacher is not so much tapping individual (and somewhat diverse) experience or (as in 3.4) encouraging students to use new vocabulary in the interpretation of events, but simply asking for literal, brief reiterations of information provided by her on earlier occasions. These kinds of teacher–pupil reviews of given knowledge have their place and their time. Teachers do need to check students' understanding of procedural, factual matters, especially where safety is involved, and this is one way of using the responses of some students to raise such matters with the whole class. But one danger of relying heavily and continuously on these traditional, formal question-and-answer reviews for guiding the construction of knowledge is that students then get little opportunity to make coherent, independent sense of what they are being taught. They are unlikely to be able to consolidate their understanding unless they have to recall and apply the relevant knowledge without the teacher's elicitations to prompt them. They also need to develop and practise their own ways of using language as a social mode of thinking, by using it to reason, argue and explain. I will return to these issues later in the book, and especially in Chapter 6.

The techniques I have described can be useful items in a teacher's linguistic tool kit. Teachers use techniques like these to help learners appreciate the relevance of their existing knowledge, to help them realize what they know, to help them see continuities in their experiences (past, present and future), and to introduce them to new knowledge in ways that allow them to make sense of it in terms of what they already know. The techniques are neither good nor bad in themselves, because it depends on how, when and why they are used. In later chapters, I will introduce some concepts which are useful for understanding this process. But now I want to present a sequence which shows how some of the techniques I have described can be used *un*successfully. It was recorded in a primary school, where a teacher was working with a group of six nine-year-olds. These were children whom the teacher considered to be of average ability or above, compared with her class as a whole. The school was one of several in the south of England in which colleagues and I made observations in the late 1980s. The sequence comes from a session in which the teacher said her aim was to help children grasp some practical rules for spelling the plurals of some English words. For anyone who has more or less mastered the system, it may be hard to remember how confusing and exasperating English spelling is for many young children, even those for whom English is their first language (as it was for the members of this group). Spelling rules therefore seem a good idea: but most attempts at them fail because of the excessive number of exceptions which have to be taken into account. One which does work quite well, however, is the rule for forming plurals of nouns ending in 'y' which have a final 'i' or 'ee' sound (such as lady, monkey, baby…). One way of expressing this rule is as follows:

If the word ends in 'vowel+y', simply add 's'. (*monkey — monkeys*)

If the word ends in 'consonant +y', delete 'y' and add 'ies'. (*lady — ladies*)

The teacher tried to teach this rule by *eliciting* it from the children, rather than simply telling them it. So for the second part of the rule she laid out a set of cards with the words 'monkey', 'donkey', 'honey' on them and asked questions as follows:

Sequence 3.6: A simple rule for spelling

Teacher: Are any of these words, letters down there vowels?

Alana: No (*Teacher turns from Alana and looks at Scott*).

Teacher: Before the 'y'?

Scott: (*long pause*) No.

Teacher: Are any of the letters before the 'y' vowels in these words?

Other pupils: Yes.

Teacher: Yes. So it's only if you've got a consonant before the vowel that you add an 'ies'. If it's a vowel before the 'y' then you still just add an 's'. So this would be — you can't have 'honeys', made a mistake or 'moneys' (*these words said very quickly and quietly*)— but you could have?

Pupils: Monkeys, donkeys… (in unison).

[*On the following day, the teacher went through a worksheet of such words with the same group children, asking specific children to provide the correct plural.*]

Teacher: Right, next one. Joanne, going down.

Joanne: You would just put an 's' on daisy because it's a continent [sic].

Teacher: Is that true? (*Addressing the rest of the group*).

Pupils: No.

Teacher: No. What would we do?

Pupils: Add 'ies'.

Teacher:	Because it makes an 'ee' sound and there's a consonant at the end.
	[*and a little later…*]
Teacher:	Right, Warren, 'banana'.
Warren:	Add 'ies'.
Teacher:	Why? Do you think we need an 'ies'? (*to Scott*)
Scott:	No.
Joanne:	Just an 's'.
Teacher:	Is it a 'y' sound that makes an 'ee' sound? (*to Scott*)
Scott:	Yes.
Robert:	No.
Teacher:	No. Is it? On 'banana'? (*pointing accusingly at Scott, who shakes his head silently*)
Teacher:	Right. So what is it we have to do?
Warren:	Add an 's' on the end.
Teacher:	Just add an 's' on the end, yes.

The remaining time in the three observed lessons was almost entirely devoted to these children doing work related to the spelling rule. They played 'matched pairs' with word cards, completing the worksheets alone or together. But the outcomes achieved were very disappointing. In a subsequent short test made up of 13 of the words used, none of the children got every plural correct (scores were 11, 9, 12, 8, 11 and 8). Surely 60 minutes of carefully prepared lessons with 6 bright children over 3 days could be expected to achieve better results?

We can see in the second part of this sequence the teacher *eliciting* information provided in the first lesson, *elaborating* the children's answers ('Because it makes an 'ee' sound'), *confirming* the correctness of some answers and *rejecting* others. What else could, or should, she have done? One possible explanation of the limited effectiveness of this bit of teaching and learning is that new knowledge was not being built upon secure existing foundations. Two essential bricks in the foundations of this knowledge were the contrastive concepts of (1) singular/plural; and (2) vowel/consonant. By the usual strategies of questioning, the teacher managed to elicit acceptable answers about singular/plural and the names of vowels from some pupils, but only from some. As I mentioned earlier, wrong answers stimulate repeated elicitations by teachers, but just one right answer and the discourse rolls on. The teacher never even asked the children about how consonants differed from vowels. (Talking to the children later, it seemed to us that only three understood both contrastive concepts.) As to the rule itself, like other similar kinds of 'procedural' knowledge, its use depends on its precise, literal recall. However, it was never presented to the children in its complete form on any occasion, and only appeared in parts in the talk of the teacher. *No-one ever wrote it down.* When we asked them, only one child could repeat the rule. (Another remembered it the wrong way round!) Perhaps because she felt she had to conform to the 'progressive' ethos of teaching in the school, the teacher actually spent very little time expounding the rule; most of the lessons were spent by the pupils either doing the oral question-and-answer routines with the teacher or working on the written activities. On this occasion, a minor 'tale of the gods' was never really told, or heard.

Summary and Conclusions

In this chapter, I have shown that the talk of teachers in schools can only be understood and evaluated in context. In principle, the roles of 'teacher' and 'learner' can be interpreted in many possible ways. In practice, however, people cannot be expected to make free interpretations of these roles because teaching and learning are shaped by cultural traditions and take place in particular social and institutional settings. Although some cultural and institutional constraints on teaching and learning may be, for all practical purposes, unquestionable and unchangeable (for example the imperative of teaching a set curriculum to large classes of learners), other conventional aspects of teaching can be questioned and changed. Comparisons between teachers, schools and cultures can help us question common-sense assumptions about how teaching and learning can be done. In every society, people who are responsible for guiding the construction of knowledge do so by using certain kinds of guidance strategies, and these include certain language *techniques* which are commonly used by teachers for developing a shared version of educational knowledge with their students. Like all techniques, of course, they carry no guarantee of success (if success is to be measured in the advanced understanding of learners). They can only be understood and evaluated as they are used, in particular settings which have their own particular contexts. We need to examine ways of guiding the construction of knowledge in terms of how well they seem suited to the kinds of learning which they are supposed to encourage.

In this chapter, I have concentrated very much on the teacher's contribution to the construction of knowledge. In the next, I will concentrate more on the contribution of the learner.

Notes

1. Rogoff, B. (1990) *Apprenticeship in Thinking*. New York: Oxford University Press.

2. Heath, S.B.(1983) *Ways with Words: Language, Life and Work in Communities and Classrooms* (p. 84). Cambridge: Cambridge University Press.
3. Munjanja, A. (1994) Unit 1: Learning from traditional education. In *Classroom Text and Discourse: A Practical Course on Language in Schools*, produced by the LITRAID Project. Harare, Zimbabwe: The Rotary Club.
4. Paradise, R. (1993) 'Passivity' in social context: Mazahua mother–child interaction. Paper presented at the seminar on Co-operation and Social Context in Adult–child and Child–child Interaction at the University of Utrecht, November 1993.
5. Philips, S. (1972) Participant structures and communicative competence. In C. Cazden, V. John and D. Hymes (eds) *The Functions of Language in the Classroom*. New York: Teachers College Press.
6. This point is well made by F. Marton (1989) in an article called 'Towards a pedagogy of content' in *Educational Psychologist* 24 (1), 1–23.
7. G.D. Jayalakshmi (1993) Video in the English curriculum of an Indian secondary school (Ph.D. thesis, The Open University).
8. G.D. Jayalakshmi (1993) p. 233.
9. G.D. Jayalakshmi (1993) p. 236.
10. Sahni, U. (1992) Literacy for empowerment. Paper presented at the First Conference for Socio-cultural Research: A research agenda for educational and cultural change. Universidad Complutense de Madrid, Spain, October 1992.
11. See Chapter 7 of Edwards, D. and Mercer, N. (1987) *Common Knowledge*. London: Methuen/Routledge.
12. See Derek Edwards' discussion of Plato's Meno in M. Billig, S. Condor, D. Edwards, M. Gane, D. Middleton and A. Radley (1988) *Ideological Dilemmas: A Social Psychology of Everyday Thinking*. London: Sage.
13. See Middleton, D. and Edwards, D. (1990) (eds) *Collective Remembering*. London: Sage. Also Rosen, H. (1993) How many genres in narrative? *Changing English* 1 (1), 179–91.
14. Brown, G. and Wragg, E. C. (1993) *Questioning*. London: Routledge.
15. See, for example, Gall, M. D. (1970) The use of questioning in teaching. *Review of Educational Research* 40, 707–21; Dillon, J. J. (1982) The multidisciplinary study of questioning. *Journal of Educational Psychology* 74, 147–65; Dillon, J. J. (1988) (ed.) *Questioning and Discussion: A Multidisciplinary Study*. London: Croom Helm. For an interesting discussion of the functions of questions in other (non-educational) kinds of conversations, see Levinson, S. (1992) Activity types and language. In P. Drew and J. Heritage (1992) (eds) *Talk at Work: Interaction in Institutional Settings*. Cambridge: Cambridge University Press.
16. Wood, D. (1986) Aspects of teaching and learning. In M. Richards and P. Light (eds) *Children of Social Worlds* (p. 209). Cambridge: Polity Press. Also see Wood, D. (1992) Teaching talk. In K. Norman (ed.) *Thinking Voices: The Work of the National Oracy Project*. London: Hodder and Stoughton. See also chapters by Mercer, Edwards, Wells and Brierley *et al.* in the same book.
17. Arthur, J. (1992) Talking like teachers: Teacher and pupil discourse in Standard Six Botswana classrooms. *Centre for Language in Social Life, Working Paper no. 26.* University of Lancaster.
18. Arthur, J. (1992) pp. 6–7.
19. The original analysis of Initiation–Response–Feedback exchanges in British schools was made by Sinclair & Coulthard (1975) *Towards an Analysis of*

Discourse: The English used by Teachers and Pupils. Oxford: Oxford University Press. A similar unit of exchange (I.R.E.) is identified in talk in North American classrooms by Mehan, H. (1979) *Learning Lessons: Social Organization in the Classroom*. Cambridge, MA: Harvard University Press. There has been some debate amongst researchers about whether these exchanges are best thought of as features of the text of talk (as Sinclair & Coulthard suggested) or features of educational practice (see Drew, P. and Heritage, J. (1992) (eds) *Talk at Work: Interaction in Institutional Settings*. Cambridge: Cambridge University Press.

20. Wood, D. (1986) pp. 211–12.
21. Barnes, D. and Todd, F. (1977) *Communication and Learning in Small Groups* (p. 116). London: Routledge & Kegan Paul.
22. From Videocassette 2, course EH232 *Computers and Learning*. Milton Keynes: Open University, 1991.
23. Dillon, J.T. (1988) *Questioning and Teaching: A Manual of Practice*. London: Croom Helm.
24. Edwards, A. D. (1992) Teacher talk and pupil competence. In Norman, K. (ed.) *Thinking Voices: The Work of the National Oracy Project* (p.238). London: Hodder & Stoughton.
25. From the video of P537 *Developing Literacy and Numeracy*, a course for trainers produced by the Open University (1989).
26. See for example Hull, R. (1985) *The Language Gap*. London: Methuen. Also hear Band 3 'Difficult Words' on the audiocassette of the 1991 INSET pack P535 *Talk and Learning 5–16*. Open University: Milton Keynes, in which two boys of 12 discuss this issue.
27. This sequence was recorded for the Open University course PE232 *Language Development*. Milton Keynes: Open University, 1979.
28. For a discussion of 'principled' and 'procedural' understanding, see Chapter 6 of Edwards, D. and Mercer, N. (1987) *Common Knowledge*. London: Methuen/Routledge.

4 The Learner's Angle

Introduction

This chapter is about how, in talk and joint activity with their teachers, learners contribute to the guided construction of knowledge. (I will leave any consideration of how learners can guide each other until Chapter 6.) Generally speaking, psychological research has tended to focus either on teaching or on learning, rather than on the development of knowledge and understanding as a joint achievement. Educational research also suggests that while teachers are often very self-critical of individuals' performance as speakers, they rarely look carefully and critically at how they and students interact. Yet the success of the process of teaching and learning depends on contributions by both teachers *and* learners. Learners are constrained, in the ways they are expected to talk and act, by their relationship with their teachers; but there are also many ways that learners influence what their teachers say and do.

How to be a 'pupil'

Research on classroom talk has tended to emphasise teachers' control of the talk and the ways that learners are constrained and limited. The classroom researcher Tony Edwards says that he sometimes offers teachers the following profile of what a child needs to do to be a competent pupil. As a pupil you have to:

- listen to the teacher, often for long periods of time;
- when the teacher stops talking, bid properly for the right to speak yourself, sometimes when competition for the next turn means balancing the risks of not being noticed against the risks of being ignored as too enthusiastic;
- answer questions to which the answer will be judged more or less relevant, useful and correct by a teacher who is seeking not to know something but to know if you know something;
- put up with having anyone's answer treated as evidence of a common understanding or misunderstanding, so that the teacher will often

explain something again when you understand it first time or rush on when you are still struggling with what was said before;

- look for clues as to what a right answer might be from the way a teacher leads into a question, and evaluates the responses — that last source of clues being often so prolific that even a wild guess may lead the teacher to answer the question for you;
- ask questions about the administration of the lesson but not usually about its content (and certainly never suggest that the teacher may be wrong);
- accept that what you know already about the topic of the lesson is unlikely to be asked for, or to be accepted as relevant, unless and until it fits into the teacher's frame of reference.[1]

Edwards comments that experienced teachers tend to receive this list 'with wry amusement', as well they might. His profile encourages us to see how contrived classroom talk is, and how constrained pupils are by it. Of course, it would not be difficult to draw up a profile for conventional success in other, relatively powerless conversational roles, such as being interviewed for a job ('Answer every question, however unreasonable or ill-informed, as though it were reasonable and well-informed'; 'Never interrupt, but gracefully yield if interrupted yourself'). Teacher–pupil interactions are a common, recognisable type of social event, and all social events require participants to follow certain rules or conventions for things to unfold in the usual, expected way.

Other taken-for-granted social conventions might also seem amusing, if stated explicitly. But one serious message of Edwards' profile is that, for much of the time in school, pupils or students are expected to follow, unquestioningly, conversational 'ground rules' which may seem to them quite arbitrary because they are imposed and never explained or justified.[2] This fact, and the nature of the rules themselves, emphasises students' relatively powerless position. As learners, their learning is continually being put on the line; one of the most distinctive characteristics of learning in school is that you are continually forced to compare your progress with that of a lot of other people. Here is a reminder from a nine-year-old boy:

Question: Can you remember what your first day at school was like?

Leslie: Horrible — I was really scared — and — and the teacher asked me a question and I couldn't answer it and another kid put up his hand and he could and it made me go all funny — inside — and I was thinking 'Oh, I couldn't do that and he could'.[3]

Given the practical, social constraints of classroom teaching, many conventional features of the traditional, 'chalk and talk' style of teacher–pupil talk are understandable and may be used to good effect. But it is clear that such talk offers learners only certain limited opportunities for using language as a social mode of thinking. Learners' opportunities for using language need to be matched with what they are trying to learn, and one of the things education is meant to develop is a capacity for applying knowledge and using language to analyse and solve problems. Trapped within the constraints of traditional teacher–pupil exchanges, learners may be spending too much time playing 'guess what's in the teacher's mind' and trying simply to 'pass' as good pupils, when they could be analysing and solving more educationally valuable kinds of problem.

However, the wit and wisdom of Edwards' profile should not blind us to the influence that pupils can and do have on the structure and content of classroom talk. Teachers may hold the power of 'gatekeepers' to curriculum knowledge and evaluators of learning, but they never have complete and conscious control over the interactions which go on in their classroom. All conversations are, to some extent, collaborative achievements, and every teacher will know of how different individuals and classes can transform the same planned lesson into radically different events. The analysis of the guided construction of knowledge is the analysis of such joint achievements.

Identity and opportunity

There are some interesting findings from research on how the social and cultural identities of students are related to their participation in classroom talk, though the picture that emerges is quite complex. There is evidence that children from some social backgrounds find public interrogations by teachers initially more strange or uncomfortable than do other children. For example, as mentioned in the previous chapter, children raised in some traditional Native American cultures seem to find the requirement of demonstrating their knowledge in front of the whole class more embarrassing than do children from middle-class Anglo-American or Western European cultures.[4] This may not be an isolated phenomenon: I have often heard university teachers remarking on how much harder it is to get British undergraduate students to talk in seminars than is the case for students in the USA. Many British teachers of children from Asian backgrounds also seem to believe that those children are naturally quieter and less demanding students than their European counterparts.[5]

But research also shows that students do not get the same *opportunities* for participation. The best-known findings on this concern the gender of the children.[6] Most teachers reliably interact more with the boys than with the girls in their class. To some extent this is caused by the fact that boys — some boys — tend to monopolise the attention of their teachers, through 'good' behaviour (like asking sensible questions) or 'bad' (i.e. misbehaving). The more active boys are therefore achieving a different kind of communicative relationship with their teachers. Research has also revealed that teachers are often unaware of the extent to which they are favouring male students with their attention. The effects of ethnicity have been less extensively researched than gender but there are findings which give serious grounds for concern. A.P. Briggs and Viv Edwards observed and recorded interactions in British primary classrooms between five teachers and the children in their classes, whom the researchers classified as either white or black (the largest ethnic minority group were of Mirpuri Pakistani origin).[7] Conscious that (as noted earlier) children of some cultural backgrounds have been observed to be more 'passive' participants in class, they compared the extent to which white or black children initiated interactions with their teacher. They found that there was no significant variation in this respect between the white and black children, or between boys and girls. However, they found that the teachers had significantly fewer interactions, and also fewer extended conversations (i.e. lasting more than 30 seconds) with black children than with white. And in line with previous research, it was found that the teachers tended to interact less with girls than boys.

To understand how both teachers and learners contribute to teaching-and-learning we need to take account of the social and cultural relationships involved. Education never takes place in a social or cultural vacuum. Schools are places with their own special kinds of knowledge and their own ways of using language, and their own power relationships; but they are part of a wider society. Teachers and students do not leave their personal and social identities outside the classroom door, and classroom talk is one means for expressing and maintaining such identities, as well as redefining them.

The Opportunities Available

In a conventional interaction between a teacher and a learner, there might seem to be just two possible ways that learners can act: they can follow the path of guidance that the teacher is offering, or they can reject, obstruct or divert it in some way. But this does no justice to what learners actually can do, or to the dynamics of classroom conversations. Think of the archetypal classroom exchange: teacher asks a question, student replies, teacher comments on reply. In 'structural' terms learners may simply be filling a 'Response' slot in an 'I–R–F' Initiation–Response–Feedback exchange (as described in Chapter 3), but the effect they have on the teacher's subsequent actions will depend on *what* they say. The meaning of the complete exchange will also depend on how the conversation has been constructed so far, and on how in turn the teacher responds. ،

Students can also respond to a teacher's guidance in different ways — enthusiastically or reluctantly, successfully or unsuccessfully. If they intentionally divert or disrupt the line that the teacher is currently trying to pursue, they can do that too in a number of significantly different ways — reasonably, humorously, maliciously, aggressively or whatever. And of course, their involvement may change over even quite short periods of time.

The next two sequences show parts of longer one-to-one conversations between a learner and a teacher. The first, Sequence 4.1, was recorded by colleagues of mine in a secondary school classroom, on an occasion when a girl (Samantha, aged 15) was talking to her teacher about a project she had been doing about her own language development. She had discussed what she saw as key points in her own language history with friends in her class, and written one and a half pages of a rather rambling narrative about her life. The teacher next wanted her to focus the content of the writing more precisely on her language development, and to organise it so that it conformed better to the style required for 'narrative' and 'descriptive' writing in the national GCSE examinations.

Sequence 4.1: A language autobiography

Teacher: Right, Samantha could you, erm, tell me how far you've got and what problems you've had? Have you gone any further than ten?

Samantha: Yeah, eleven, and, like, when I just come, like left Beechside, my previous school, come to this school and where I met Angela again from where I met her up at the hospital and that and…erm, then I met her friend, Sharon, now we're friends again.

Teacher: And what language bit are you talking about there when you're meeting up with your new friends, with your old friends?

Samantha: Well, I knew Angela from like when my nan used to go up the hospital and that and have check-ups, but I didn't know Sharon until I come to this school and until Angela introduced me to her, that was when I was eleven.

Teacher: So it's part of your language biography you've described there, your meeting up with those friends again. What points are you going to make after that? You're going to be looking at your vocabulary or looking at the way you talk with friends?

Samantha: Yeah, in a way, in a way I acted in some of my lessons and that and how I acted against, erm, like books when I first come to this school cos I didn't really like them. (*Pause*) I'm not sure if I've got enough from nought to one.

Teacher: Right, OK. Can you just read the start there, and I'll listen to see how it sounds, OK?

Samantha: What to that bit?

Teacher: Well, is that where your first paragraph's gonna come to an end?

Samantha: Yeah. I think so, cos there's, like, what I'm talking about how, what about my mum and dad and that and my family and I go on to how I, how I learned to speak and that.

Teacher: Right, OK. So test that out, see what it sounds like. (*Samantha reads*)

Teacher: What are you so worried about putting that at the beginning, why would I think, do you think, that is a good start?

Samantha: I dunno, I think it's a bit of a mouthful in some ways.

Teacher: Why is it important to, why have you decided to put all that in there about your mum and dad, what's that say about you?

Samantha: It's sort of tell em why I'm a bit sort of cockney accent and that and shows, erm, like what sort of background I've sort of had off of my parents.[8]

In terms of its structure, Sequence 4.1 has many of the characteristics of a traditional teacher–pupil interaction. The teacher asks a lot of questions. We can see that he is pursuing some specific teaching aims through the conversation — we know that he thinks that the topic of language development needs to be made more explicit in her piece, and he is also trying to guide her towards the ground rules which apply in GCSE writing. He continually tries to relate what she has already said to these two sets of criteria. Notice, however, that Samantha persistently side-steps her teacher's questions, answering them in a way which re-establishes her own agenda (which seems to highlight other aspects of her life such as where and when she met her friends). It is clear that both parties are influencing the course of this conversation; but it might also seem that, in terms of guiding the construction of knowledge, the conversation is getting no-where.

The eventual outcome of the conversation, however, was one of the best and longest pieces of writing that Samantha did for her GCSE English course. Parts of the final version of her autobiography were still about events which, while they had obviously deeply influenced her, were not related to language as explicitly as the teacher thought that they should be. It seemed, however, that these elements were essential for Samantha's own commitment to writing this piece — this was what she *wanted* to write about and so she did. But she did include enough appropriate content and structured her writing well enough overall to achieve a grade which was much better than for her previous assignments. She could not have done this without responding to her teacher's help. On the other hand, her teacher told the researchers that he avoided being too strongly directive because he understood that autobiography is a sensitive topic. In the past he had found that Samantha was resistant to criticisms of her writing and if she became discouraged was likely to give up altogether. As a joint outcome, Samantha's improved grade was a tribute to his sensitivity as well as his expert knowledge. The educational quality of this language event can only really be understood in the context of a continuing communicative relationship between a teacher and a learner.

Appreciating the learner's angle on classroom conversations means also recognising that learners have their own interpretations of events and may be following their own agendas. Every teacher will have experienced occasions when their agenda and those of students have become impossible to reconcile. (The experience of too many such occasions over a short time is a good stimulus for a change of career!) This book is not about disorderly behaviour, and I will not be including any examples of teachers and learners in violent conflict in this chapter. Instead, I have tried to find some sequences of talk which illustrate the kinds of opportunities that learners have for exerting their influence over the direction that a classroom conversation takes. The next sequence comes from a secondary school in the English midlands which I have visited several times. It involves a 15-year-old secondary pupil who had, in a 'work experience' capacity, been spending some of her school time helping in an elderly persons' social club attached to the school. She is talking to her class tutor.

Sequence 4.2: Not a normal schoolday

Teacher: Well, you've been working now, you've been going to the frail elderly, helping that for nearly half a term now haven't you?

Donna: Yeh.

Teacher: So I was wondering about whether you might think now might be perhaps be a good time to start to write something down about, about it.

Donna: Don't know, it would make it seem more like work than fun, wouldn't it? Make it more like a normal schoolday, because I enjoy it so much.

Teacher: But for your final folder, for social sciences, it would make a really good project wouldn't it? It would look pretty good in the folder if you could put something together like that.

Donna: I think it would change my attitude while I was there. It'd feel like I was interviewing them or something.

Donna is clearly rejecting her teacher's attempt to 'educationalise' her work experience, to treat it as a resource for conventional educational achievement. There is a conflict between Donna's perceptions of the value of this experience and those of her teacher, and this conflict is being acted out in the talk. An essential element of the role of the teacher in school is to help students make an education out of their experience, and Donna's reaction would seem to stop the guided construction process in its tracks (for the moment, at least). Understandable as it may seem, her reaction seems a sad reflection of the psychological boundaries which commonly emerge between 'educational knowledge' and 'the rest of life'. Certainly there is something distinctive about the content of much educational knowledge. But the kinds of analytic and expressive skills which education is also meant to develop are not necessarily antithetical to personal involvement, purpose and enjoyment, as many writers, researchers and members of various professions could testify. In fact, a common complaint in those professions (and in many other trades and industries) today is that the education system is sending them new recruits who lack such skills. Perhaps Donna's reaction supports the view that too little time is spent explicitly linking the discourses of education to those of the rest of life.

There is, however, another possible and more positive interpretation of Sequence 4.2. When I talked to Donna's teacher after the recording, he seemed less disappointed than I might have expected about how the conversation had gone. He knew Donna well, and was aware of the low value she attached to academic achievement. Her current life-plans ran in directions which made it seem irrelevant, and she would soon be leaving school. But he also said for him that the recorded conversation demonstrated that the school *had* helped Donna develop the kinds of assertiveness and communication skills which were valuable in the modern world — she represented her position clearly and calmly, and justified her views. The conversation was a model of rational debate, in which two people presented their positions, accounted for them, and agreed to differ. [9] He also felt that it confirmed the quality of the relationship he had established with her, within which she felt able to speak her mind.

Like Sequence 4.1, Sequence 4.2 shows how any sequence of classroom talk is just a snapshot — it needs to be put back into its time and its context to be properly understood and evaluated. A conversation between a teacher and learner is one stretch of the road from the history of their particular teaching-and-learning relationship into its future. Edwards and Westgate make a similar point using the next sequence, which was also recorded in an English secondary school. It shows how, with an enviable talent for repartee, a student turns the conversation along the route of her choice.

Teacher: Mmm, well, do you know Tracey, it hurts me to say it, but for you — it's not a bad piece of work.

Tracey: Gee, thanks.

Teacher: No, I mean, just think, if you really got stuck in — you know, really tried — you could be almost average.

Tracey: Who'd want to be like you anyway?

Pupils: Come off it, sir, she'd never make average.

Tracey: Hey, if I was average, bird-brains, I'd be top of this class.

Teacher: (*Laughing*) If you were average, you wouldn't be in this class.

Pupils: (*Laughing*) Nice one, Porky, nice one.

Tracey: You must be a not-average teacher, having us.

Teacher: Dead right, I'm not average.

Tracey: That's what I said.

Teacher: (*Laughing*) Right — one to you.

Tracey: You can't count either.[10]

Is this an example of disruption in the educational process, or does it illustrate the quality of the personal relationship which this particular teacher had developed with a group of learners? This is a difficult sort of question for a researcher, who normally shares only a brief time with the people being observed and has very limited access to their shared past experience. As Edwards and Westgate say, 'Repartee trades on common knowledge, not only of particular events in past encounters which are referred to obliquely, but also of the conventions which mark off permissible humour from humour which has "gone too far"' (p. 96). Such things may be hard to research, but they provide the interpersonal, emotional basis for the guided construction of knowledge.

An interesting illustration of how humour and repartee can be formally incorporated into teaching and learning comes from the traditional Zimbabwean ways of educating children which I referred to in the previous chapter. In rural village communities, one way that girls are educated for their adult life is through conversations with an older aunt or grandmother. Sometimes, these conversations consist of an older woman addressing a whole group of girls, say while they are sitting by the fire in the evening. While most of this conversation may consist of the aunt telling them of things they should know and do, there is an opportunity for one of the older girls to act as a provocatrice, to question the aunt's wisdom, as in this example (translated from the Shona) which was video-taped for an in-service course for teachers. The older woman and a group of about 12 girls are sitting round a fire in the open air of the evening. The older woman (who I will call 'Aunt') has been speaking to them about their future adult lives.

Aunt: Now girls, do you understand what I mean?

Girls: (*in unison*) Yes.

Aunt: We want you girls to have good manners, to be respected wherever you go (*an older girl gets up and starts to poke the fire*). Why are you kindling the fire? Leave it alone! How can you do that while I talk?

Girl: Does it matter, grandmother?

Aunt: That's what I mean about not having any manners (*all laugh*).

Girl: I'm just improving the fire.

Aunt: (*to the older girl*) By the way, is there any water here?

Girl: No, there is none.

Aunt: Why must you always be sent to the well?

Girl: Whoever wants water should go and fetch it herself.

Aunt: No, no, no! (*emphatically shaking her forefinger*). When you are married you must not wait for someone to send you.

Girl: So how can I cope with working for all of them?

Aunt: Yes, if you are in your mother-in-law's house you will have to work.

Girl: That won't do. We shall have to do it together (*smiling*).

Aunt: With who?

Girl: With the mother-in-law.

Aunt: (*gestures apparently with exasperation*) That's when you get confused. You should wait for her to say 'My daughter-in-law, rest'. Now that's when you rest. Do not fight with the owner of the home.

Girl: We will just have to do that.

Aunt: You must not (*again emphasising with her finger*) go to your mother-in-law's house and say that you can't cope. Do you understand what I am saying girls?

Girls: (*in unison*) Yes.[11]

This is a language event with a neat, symmetrical form. The aunt offers a home truth, the girls confirm that they hear it. The provocatrice then questions this wisdom, the aunt reasserts it; and the girls then again confirm that they have heard. It seems that everyone involved knows how to make this kind of event happen — everyone involved seems to know the 'ground rules' for how to talk and act. There is humour involved, but this contributes to the construction of knowledge rather than obstructing it.

The learners provide a rather different and more varied kind of contribution to a classroom conversation in the next sequence, which comes from Janet Maybin's research on formal and informal talk in British primary schools. In it, we can see Julie, Kirsty and Sharon (10 years old) working together while also interacting with the teacher and a parent-helper (Mrs Reilly). Julie is drawing a live snail on a card, to put up in a classroom display, and Kirsty and Mrs Reilly have come back from the library with a book about snails. Julie is also simultaneously helping another child ('Pupil' in the extract) to do a word puzzle in a magazine. (Note: / shows an interruption, [shows people speaking at the same time and ... shows where speech was indecipherable.)

Julie:	I'll just write 'This was drawn by bla bla bla'.
Kirsty:	It's got thousands of teeth. (*reads*) 'Its long tongue is covered with thousands of tiny teeth'. He's got thousands of teeth.
Julie:	He has, he's got thousands of teeth, that little snail has.
Sharon:	Look at its trail (*teacher comes over*).
Julie:	Miss, it's got hundreds and...it's got thousands and thousands of teeth/
Kirsty:	/on its long tongue.
Teacher:	It's got what?
Kirsty:	Thousands of teeth. It says here.
Mrs Reilly:	Those are tentacles. It's got four tentacles.
Julie:	Yea, teeth, teeth.
Mrs Reilly:	(*reads*): 'to touch, feel and smell, and it breathes through [the hole in its side'.
Julie:	[teeth.
Mrs Reilly:	So there must be a hole somewhere.
Julie:	'eat' (*a suggestion to the pupil with the puzzle magazine*).
Mrs Reilly:	We saw its eyes, didn't we? At the end of its tentacles and it can only see light and dark.
Julie:	(*to puzzle magazine pupil*) 'tune'.
Pupil:	it can only be three letters/.
Julie:	/(reads) 'or more'. Three letters or more.
Kirsty:	Miss it's got a thousand — thousands of teeth on its tongue.

Sharon:	Yes, cause we went into the library. Mrs Reilly and Kirsty went into the library to look it up.
Teacher:	What's that, the snail?
Sharon:	Yea.
Pupil:	Miss, where's the sellotape?
Kirsty:	And it breathes through its side.
Kirsty:	It breathes [through...its side.
Sharon:	[it's got this little hole/
Kirsty:	/It breathes through a hole in its side.[12]

This conversation is an excellent illustration of how complicated conversational life often is in the primary school classroom. It shows three pupils contributing actively and enthusiastically to the 'official' discourse of the classroom, even though one of them also successfully carries on a parallel 'unofficial' conversation. But it also shows people using talk to try to create an *educational* event out of their shared experience. The girls share observations they think are significant, and they emphasise their joint recognition of this significance in two interesting ways: (i) *repeating* each other's comments ('thousands of teeth'...'it breathes through its side') and (ii) constructing some comments *together* ('...thousands of teeth...on its long tongue'.) Adults and children refer to the authority of a book for interpreting their experience. The children involved do not appear to be unduly constrained, but the guidance of the adults is quite apparent. However, as Maybin points out, there also seems to be something of a struggle between the different ways of contributing to this conversation. Mrs Reilly tries to encourage the girls to use the book to guide their perceptions of the snail ('it breathes through the hole in its side...So there must be a hole somewhere'). Her way of talking is self-consciously 'scientific', a model of the scientific ways of talking and learning that the children are being encouraged to adopt.[13] But the girls seem more interested in picking out striking items of information for presentation to the teacher, and they use these to vie with each other for her attention. Their talk, then, seems to reflect their aim of presenting themselves to their teacher as good pupils.

Changing Opportunities

Classroom talk is shaped by many factors, and changes in some aspects of classroom organisation may have unexpected effects on the ways learners contribute to conversations with their teacher. The next sequence comes from the research in Indian secondary schools by G. D. Jayalakshmi which I introduced in the previous chapter. Jayalakshmi found that the introduction of video-led, small group activity seemed to cause a shift in power between teacher and pupils, with the teacher's position as the authoritative source of knowledge being undermined. One source of her evidence for this was an increase in the number of disruptive contributions to the talk by pupils. For example, on this occasion the pupils sat in groups while the teacher wrote on the board. They were discussing how heat is produced.

Teacher: Now heat is produced by...Group Number 1.
Janardhan: By burning coal, oil, electricity.
Vishu: (*adding to the list*) Gas.
Teacher: And? (*starts writing on blackboard*) Heat is produced by coal.
Many voices: By burning coal sir, by burning coal.
Teacher: (*continues writing on blackboard*) Heat is produced by coal, oil,
Prashant: (*taking the mickey*) Water.
Teacher: Water.
Asutosh: (*to members of his group*) By burning water? (*Group starts laughing*)
Many students: (*obviously enjoying themselves*) Burning water, burning water.
Teacher: Heat is produced by coal, oil, water.
Jayant: (*taking pity on him*) No sir, not water.
Teacher: (*a bit sheepish?*) No water (*rubs it out from board*) OK, I keep it in doubt.[14]

Jayalakshmi comments, 'the students here obviously feel more confident in their own answers and abilities and so can challenge the teacher as well as tease him. This was quite unthinkable in the traditional lessons'. That is, the conversational ground rules which had applied in the traditional lessons were being tested and broken by the pupils. The teacher, on his part, appeared to offer no defence of the rules or any justification to the students for why the rules should continue to be upheld.

Much more encouraging experiences, from a teacher's point of view at least, can also come from change. Irene Shantry, a British teacher, describes how she experimented with changing the conversational ground rules in her primary school classroom:

My awareness of the value of adopting the role of 'non-expert' grew out of a small classroom incident. While writing out an address, I said, half to myself, 'Is that how you spell Jamaica?' Then I turned to the group of five- and six-year-old children with me and said, laughingly, 'I can't spell Jamaica. Can you?' The response was immediate: 'I can'; 'So can I'; 'I can, my aunty lives in Jamaica'; 'It's in the story'. There was a rush to the book area and several hands presented me with the book *Jamaica's Find* by Juanita Havill.

I decided to build on this enthusiasm and discussed with the children the problem I had with many other words. I presented myself as a learner, thereby creating the situation where they felt that they had to do something to help me. The children shared with me some of the methods they had learned to enable them to deal with spelling. For example, to spell 'friend', simply take the first bit of 'Friday' from the class calendar and add 'end'. Another child showed me how a dictionary could be a valuable asset. From that point on, I decided to change the emphasis of my questioning strategy. 'How would...?' became 'I wonder how...?', on the premise that the way a question is asked is as important as the actual question...

I believe that this 'non-expert' approach is a very positive way of developing children's learning. It creates relationships of trust and co-operation, The children's response is very different from that to more evaluative questioning. They take the initiative more frequently; are no longer hesitant about speaking and are less anxious about putting themselves in the limelight. They work out the answer together and enjoy the responsibility of helping the teacher.[15]

Shantry's inspiration for this change, it seems, was the critical research on teachers' questions mentioned in Chapter 3. After admitting her own perplexity about a spelling (thus following one of the suggestions made by Tony Edwards, listed on page 32), she deliberately maintained the role of 'non-expert' and did so for clear and justifiable reasons (in order to encourage the children to take more initiative, to develop more confidence in speaking and to work together to solve problems). From a more detached point of view, one can see some problems in Shantry's claim that her pretence of ignorance could be the basis for a 'relationship of trust'; but she and her colleagues were not unaware of this issue. The key change was a temporary role-reversal, allowing the children to feel that they were guiding the construction of her knowledge. The new questioning strategy was a technique for achieving this, which worked *in context* because of the things she asked about and the circumstances in which she did so. This encouraged the children to express their knowledge and understanding in such a way that it would be useful to someone else — that 'someone' very unusually being their teacher. As well as giving the teacher some insights into their knowledge, this kind of opportunity may well have helped the pupils develop their own understanding. (I know that I only feel confident that I really understand something when I can explain it properly to someone else.[16])

Having looked at teachers in Chapter 3 and at learners in this chapter, to be true to my own socio-cultural perspective I now need to put them back together. For the last sequence in this chapter, I want to look at an occasion where some learners exerted considerable influence over the content and direction of the talk, but the teacher nevertheless directed the conversation in such a way that he achieved his desired educational outcomes. I recorded it in a British primary classroom in 1990. In the sequence the teacher is talking with a group of six children aged nine who are reading together a picture book for children called *I'll Take You to Mrs Cole* by Nigel Gray. The teacher told me that this group included children who had severe problems with reading, and with 'making sense of books'. One of the teacher's main aims in this discussion was therefore to help the children understand the kinds of meanings that literary language could convey. He had also been influenced by reading Matthew Lipman's [17] work on developing children's 'thinking skills' and so a second aim was to encourage children to provide clear explanations, to share ideas and to argue rationally about possible solutions to problems. Some of the children in this particular group were very shy, and usually silent, in larger class settings (including Terry, the boy who talks most in the transcribed sequence), and the teacher also used this kind of discussion to help develop their communicative confidence. At the point the sequence begins, they are talking about an illustration in the book in which the hero (a boy) seems to appear twice. There has been some disagreement amongst the children about quite who these two figures are meant to represent.

My suggestion is that you read through the sequence and form your own preliminary views about what is going on in terms of teaching and learning. Then read my own analysis (which follows) and see if you find it convincing. (Note that P1 and P2 refer to children whom I was unable to identify.)

Sequence 4.3: 'Perhaps'

Teacher:	Which one's the boy in the story then?
P1:	That one.
P2:	That one (*both pupils speak together*).
Teacher:	Why do you say that?
P1:	'Cause he's got spiky hair and he's wearing long trousers.
Teacher:	Sarah disagrees. Why not?
Sarah:	It can't be the boy because he's not got spiky hair.

	(*Some of the children begin talking at once*)
Terry:	(*loudly*) No, he's thinking again, he's not gone to Mrs Cole yet.
Teacher:	Hold on, remember, one at a time please. Sorry?
Terry:	He's thinking again, that's why he's got 'perhaps, perhaps she kept'.
Teacher:	Ah.
Terry:	He's thinking what it's like.
Teacher:	He's thinking what it's like. So is he actually in this picture (*points to one of the scenes shown*).
Terry:	No.
Sarah:	No.
Teacher:	What part of him is in the picture?
Terry:	His mind.
Sarah:	Yeh, his mind's in the picture.
Teacher:	How can a mind get into a picture?
Sarah:	Ima...Thinking about it.
Terry:	Yeh.
	[*The discussion continues and then...*]
Teacher:	Let's go back. It's interesting isn't it? First of all, let's reflect on this a minute. First of all, some people thought, somebody thought that he was in there...
P1:	Yeh.
P2:	Yeh.
Teacher:	...and then Terry disagreed with that, or Sarah, is it? And then we said, what part of him is in there, and you said his mind, right? So this (*points to the picture*) is his mind still, is it? And Terry picked up a clue from the writing that made him think of the mind. What word was it Terry that gave you that idea about it being in his mind?
Terry:	Well, in the writing...
Teacher:	Yeh.
Terry:	...bit. 'Perhaps', it said, 'perhaps she kept them locked up in dark // dungeon'.
T:	So 'perhaps', 'perhaps'. Was that the key word for you?
Terry:	Yeh.
T:	'Perhaps'. It goes on to say 'perhaps', doesn't it ? (*Reads from page*) 'Perhaps she fed them' (*long pause, children look at the book*). It's still all in his mind, is it?
Sarah:	Yeh.[18]

The content of this sequence depends heavily on the contributions of learners. At the point it begins, the main conversational issue (whether or not an illustration shows the hero of the story) is one that had been raised by the children in the group. The eventual clue to its resolution also comes from one of them (Terry). But of course the teacher's contributions are very significant. He picks up the issue, and uses some of the techniques I described in Chapter 3 (summarised in Table 1 on page 34) to get the children to consider the problem more carefully. He *elicits* their views of the problem, which not only tells him what they think but also helps the group share ideas. He *repeats* some of the remarks they make, holding them up to the group and showing that he thinks that they have special educational significance ('He's thinking what it's like'). He notices that Terry may have got an idea from the text which would resolve the issue. After helping the children clarify their ideas (by asking questions like 'What part of him is in the picture?', 'How can a mind get into a picture?' and 'What word was it Terry that gave you that idea?') he *recaps* the discussion ('Let's go back...First of all...') and so tries to provide a firm context based on shared experience within which Terry can represent his 'clue'. Finally, the teacher *elaborates* the conclusion that had eventually been reached ('It's still all in his mind, is it?'). Through the teacher's actions, Terry's discovery is made explicit and legitimised, and what he has found becomes part of the shared understanding, the collective consciousness of the group. This discussion became an *educational* event because of the teacher's interventions, many of which took the form of questions. The teacher's own comments on his interventions in such discussions were as follows:

> On the one hand, it is necessary to be very flexible and adaptable in one's thinking, watching out for and reacting entirely to issues and interpretations raised by the children. On the other hand, the teacher has a responsibility for encouraging and maintaining the philosophical, enquiring nature of the dialogue.[19]

Summary and Conclusions

While, in Chapter 3, I described ways that teachers tried to guide learning through talking to learners, in this chapter I have looked at some kinds of opportunities that learners have for active involvement in conversations with their teachers. (I have deliberately avoided much consideration of how learners can talk and learn together in the absence of their teacher, because that is the main topic of Chapter 6.) All the evidence from research tells us that, in most classrooms, the range of opportunities for learners to contribute to talk is quite narrow and the amount of talk they contribute is relatively small. From an educational point of view, there are some good reasons for being critical of this state of affairs. As much as anything, education ought to be a means for helping learners develop ways of using language as a social mode of thinking, and this is hardly likely to be successful if their opportunities for using language are limited to narrow response slots in conversations with teachers.[20]

Nevertheless, I have shown how learners can and do influence the course of the guided construction of knowledge, even under quite conventional and constrained circumstances. The emphasis of much past research on the power and control exerted by teachers may have tended to make us overlook these contributions and underestimate their actual and potential significance. I have tried to show how the ways that learners talk with their teachers and the ways that talk contributes to their learning cannot be understood simply by identifying specific features and conventional patterns of classroom talk. In classroom talk, as in all conversations, we see people asserting their own agendas and representing their own interests. We also see them attempting to establish shared agendas and perspectives and pursuing joint interests. It may also be possible to discern the influence of broader, cultural influences and values. Most teachers and learners have continuing relationships; their conversations are built upon a shared history and (in the short to medium term, at least) are working towards a joint future. As a researcher, I only sample teaching-and-learning relationships at some point in their development. Even if I visit participants over some days or weeks (which, in my own research, is what I try to do) I know that they have a communicative history and future, of which I can only ever see traces in the continuous present that I share with them. It is to remind us of such things that we need to take a historical, social and cultural perspective on the guided construction of knowledge. We need a suitable theory of the process, and that is what I am concerned with in the next chapter.

Notes

1. Edwards, A. D. (1992) Teacher talk and pupil competence. In Norman, K. (ed.) *Thinking Voices: The Work of the National Oracy Project* (pp. 235–6). London: Hodder & Stoughton.
2. See Willes, M. (1983) *Children into Pupils: A Study of Language in Early Schooling.* London: Routledge & Kegan Paul. For more detailed discussion of 'educational ground rules', see Edwards, D. and Mercer, N. (1987) *Common Knowledge* (Chapter 4). London: Methuen/Routledge; and Sheeran, Y. and Barnes, D. (1991) *School Writing: Discovering the Ground Rules.* Milton Keynes: Open University Press.
3. Martin, T. (1986) Leslie: A reading failure talks about failing. In N. Mercer (ed.) *Language and Literacy from an Educational Perspective: Volume 2, In Schools* (p. 180). Milton Keynes: Open University Press.
4. See the references to research by Paradise (1993) and Philips (1972) in Chapter

3 (notes 4 and 5). Also Van Ness, H. (1982) Social control and social organisation in an Athabaskan classroom: A micro-ethnography of getting ready for reading. In H. Tueba, G. Guthrie and K. Au (eds) *Culture in the Bilingual Classroom*. Rowley, MA: Newbury House.

5.   Brah, A. and Minhas, R. (1988) Structural racism or cultural difference: Schooling for Asian girls. In M. Woodhouse and A. McGrath (eds) *Family, School and Society*. London: Hodder & Stoughton.

6.   Swann, J. (1992) *Girls, Boys and Language*. London: Blackwell; and Swann, J. (1994) What do we do about gender? In B. Stierer and J. Maybin (eds) *Language, Literacy and Learning in Educational Practice*. Clevedon: Multilingual Matters.

7.   Biggs, A. P. and Edwards, V. (1994) I treat them all the same: Teacher–pupil talk in multi-ethnic classrooms. In D. Graddol, J. Maybin and B. Stierer (eds) *Researching Language and Literacy in Social Context*. Clevedon: Multilingual Matters.

8.   Sequence 4.1 comes from Videocassette 4 of the Open University course E271 *Curriculum and Learning*, but I am indebted to Janet Maybin and Barry Stierer for the analysis of this sequence (see Maybin, Mercer and Stierer, 1992).

9.   Of course, the teacher's later conversation with me cannot be treated as an 'explanation' for Sequence 4.2. It is simply another conversation for analysis, in which a teacher is making himself professionally accountable for his practice. (For further discussion of this notion of 'accountability' in conversations, see Mercer, N. and Longman, J. (1992) Accounts and the development of shared understanding in Employment Training Interviews, *Text* 12 (1), pp. 103–25; Edwards, D. and Potter, J. (1992) *Discursive Psychology*. London: Sage.)

10. This sequence comes from O'Connor, T. (1983) Classroom humour (Unpublished B.Phil. thesis, Newcastle University), as quoted in Edwards, A. D. and Westgate, D. (1987) *Investigating Classroom Talk* (pp. 96–97). London: The Falmer Press.

11. From 'TV Programme 1: Patterns in traditional learning', *Classroom Text and Discourse: A Practical Course on Language in Schools*, produced by the LITRAID Project. Harare, Zimbabwe: The Rotary Club.

12. From Maybin, J. (1994) Children's voices: Talk, knowledge and identity. In D. Graddol, J. Maybin and B. Stierer (eds) *Researching Language and Literacy in Social Context* (p. 136). Clevedon: Multilingual Matters.

13. See Lemke, J.L. (1990) *Talking Science: Language, Learning and Values*. Norwood, NJ: Ablex.

14. G. D. Jayalakshmi (1993) Video in the English Curriculum of an Indian secondary school (pp. 281–2). Ph.D. thesis, The Open University.

15. From Brierley, L., Cassar, I., Loader, P., Norman, K., Shantry, I., Wolfe, S. and Wood, D. (1992) No, we ask you questions. In K. Norman (ed.) *Thinking Voices: The Work of the National Oracy Project*. London: Hodder & Stoughton.

16. There is some evidence from research to support the idea that simply talking about a problem or task makes learning more effective. See for example Fletcher, B. (1985) Group and individual learning of junior school children on a microcomputer-based task, *Educational Review* 37, pp. 251–61.

17. Lipman, M. (1970) *Philosophy for Children*. Montclair, NJ: Institute for the Advancement of Philosophy for Children.

18. Sequence 4.5 is transcribed in more detail on pp. A8–A9 of Mercer, N. (1991)

Learning through talk. In P535 *Talk and Learning 5–16*. Milton Keynes: The Open University.

19. Prentice, M. (1991) A community of enquiry. In P535 *Talk and Learning 5–16*. Milton Keynes: The Open University.

20. Support for the benefits of balancing teacher-led discussions with other kinds of language activities, and also for the importance of teacher control in the organisation of classroom talk, is provided by the results of Ann Brown and Annemarie Palincsar's experimental 'reciprocal teaching' programme. The programme, focusing on the development of reading comprehension, is explicitly based on a socio-cultural model of teaching and learning. See Brown, A. and Palincsar, A.S. (1989) Guided, cooperative learning and individual knowledge acquisition. In L. Resnick (ed.) *Knowing, Learning and Instruction*. New York: Lawrence Erlbaum.

5 A Theory of Practice

Introduction

This chapter is a sketch for a theory of how talk is used to guide the construction of knowledge in schools and other educational institutions. By 'theory' I mean a simplified, explanatory model of the process I have been describing in the book so far: teaching and learning carried out through talk in classrooms. We do not have a satisfactory theory of this process, in my opinion, though research has provided some excellent resources for building one. Later in the chapter, I will list what I believe are the essential requirements for this theory, and then suggest how the requirements can be met. But first, I will explain why I think such a theory is needed by both researchers and teachers.

Theories have to simplify real life, in order to explain it. They are meant to enable us to see the wood for the trees, the patterns of relationship and causality in events. As a researcher, I need a theory of the guided construction of knowledge to make sense of my observations. But another good reason for developing such a theory is to help people who are responsible for the quality of that process, such as teachers, develop and maintain a critical awareness of what they do. In any applied field, theories are intended to guide practical judgements and steer new developments. They can help practitioners share understanding, so that they have more than hearsay evidence and personal experience upon which to plan and evaluate their activities. In 1982, a group of British teachers published a book called *Becoming Our Own Experts* which, amongst other things, deals with the relationship between theory and practice. They say: 'Our theory, our "expertise", is in making sensitive inferences about an actual classroom experience, in noticing what is really going on. If the expert in the more usual sense, who stands back a little from the everyday reality of the classroom in order, ideally, to get a wider view of the scene, has a role in this process of discovery, it is simply to help the classroom teacher to discover more fully what is already there. Unrelated theory has no value in this context; it will quite rightly be dumped by the teacher as excess baggage'.[1] I am a teacher myself, and I know from my own experience and my involvement with other teachers that this is true. A good theory of the guided construction of knowledge ought to serve the needs of both researchers and practitioners.

Theory Under Attack

In the world of education, theories of the process of teaching and learning can be very important. Strangely enough, this is illustrated by the fact that 'educational theory' has been given such rough treatment in recent years by various politicians, journalists and other self-appointed guardians of 'educational standards'. In Britain, in particular, this has been part of a sustained attack on 'progressive' and 'child-centred' approaches to education (particularly in the primary sector) which were developed in the 1960s and 70s.[2] The rhetoric of these attacks usually offers a simplistic choice; on the one hand we have 'theory' (pie-in-the-sky ideas which are ideologically loaded, which ignore the common-sense realities of the 'real world', and so on) and on the other 'practice' (the actual job of teaching, which can be done in a straightforward, no-nonsense way, and which is best learnt simply by doing it).

But 'theory' is not the real target of those attacks. What is really being attacked is a set of beliefs about how children learn, how they should be taught, and what they should be taught. The idea that there can be educational policy and practice without a theory of some kind is simply nonsense. The choice is always between one theory and another, even if the theories involved are never clearly spelled out. By attacking the 'theory' of progressive education, critics are implying that they have a better understanding of how and what children should be taught. This means that they must have, at some level, a theory of their own. Most critics of progressive education never make their theory explicit, or bother to relate it to observations of what actually goes on in classrooms. Yet they use their theory implicitly to assert that classroom education is best done by teachers who stand at the front doing most of the talking, that organising 'group work' and talk amongst students is probably just a waste of time, and that students' learning is best evaluated through the frequent use of formal written tests. It seems that for them, choices are always quite straightforward: education can either be of the 'loose', progressive, child-centred, discovery-learning kind, or it can be run along the traditional lines of an efficiently organised, 'back-to-basics', no-nonsense Victorian classroom. Rhetoric of this kind can itself be studied and analysed as an attempt to use language to guide people's thinking. By presenting social problems as having certain obvious causes, by transforming causes into blame which can be attached to some relatively powerless social groups (e.g. educational theorists, teachers, one-parent families...) and by describing the issues in suitably moralistic and emotional terms, this establishes a convenient interpretation of events — a 'moral panic' which identifies the villains and exonerates those in power.[3]

In the end, it is not really theories of education that figure in the heated debates about classroom practice, but educational *ideologies* — belief systems which, while implicitly invoking some theory of teaching and learning, also implicitly invoke cultural, political and moral values. Unlike theories, ideologies cannot really be tested or disproved. The re-assertion of a traditional, 'back to basics' approach to classroom education over a progressive, 'child-centred' one would not be a triumph of 'practice' over 'theory' but rather the shifting of the basis of classroom practice from one ideology of teaching and learning to another. This should not happen: theories need to be brought out into the open, so that they can be evaluated. This is why we need a good theory of the guided construction of knowledge. There are ways of understanding the process of education which can help teachers avoid the stark choice between the 'traditional' and the 'progressive', as I hope to show.

Three essential requirements for a socio-cultural theory of the guided construction of knowledge

A theory of the guided construction of knowledge in schools and other educational settings must do three closely related things. It must:

(i)   explain how language is used to create joint knowledge and under-standing;

(ii) explain how people help other people to learn;

(iii) take account of the special nature and purpose of formal education.

I will go on to discuss some concepts which could help us build a theory to these requirements.

Talk and the Construction of Knowledge

Back in Chapter 1, I suggested that we need to recognise that knowledge exists as a social entity and not just as an individual possession. To think of 'knowledge' only as an individual mental possession does not do justice to the capabilities of human beings. The essence of human knowledge and understanding is that it *is* shared. Every generation in every society builds upon the cultural foundations of previous ones, and every new discovery only really comes into existence when it is communicated. This is the essence of what I called the *socio-cultural approach* to the study of the development of knowledge and understanding. In contrast to most earlier psychological approaches to learning and thinking, it gives explicit recognition to how people construct knowledge together. This inevitably highlights the role of language in the construction of knowledge. Individually and collectively, we use language to transform experience into knowledge and understanding. It provides us with both an individual and a social mode of thinking.

Talk as social action

However, the idea of a 'social mode of thinking', for all its value, has a somewhat meditative feel to it. We should not forget that in the classroom, as in other places, talk is used *to get things done*. In recent years, within linguistics, psychology and sociology, there has been increasing interest in talk as social action.[4] This research encourages us to see that in classroom talk, as in other kinds of conversation, people use language to pursue their interests and goals. They want to get somewhere, and their conversations are vehicles for doing so. Speakers in a conversation may not have shared goals, common purposes, or the same understandings of experiences; I gave some examples in earlier chapters (especially in Chapter 4) of instances where it seemed that teachers and learners did not share the same goals. But they can strive to achieve these, if they wish, through talk and joint action. Look back, for example, to Sequence 2.3 *Maximum Box* on page 12. There we see a group of girls working towards a joint understanding through argument. The creation of shared knowledge and understanding is rarely, if ever, a matter of simply pooling information. Information can be accumulated, but knowledge and understanding are only generated by *working* with information, selecting from it, organising it, arguing for its relevance. People use talk to *account for* the opinions they hold and the information they provide.

So in classroom talk, as in talk elsewhere, we see people working out what they know, and achieving what they can. But of course, speakers do not, cannot, say everything they know. People will try to say things that they think are relevant and appropriate to that situation. They may have reasons for not revealing what they know — teachers may withhold explanations because they want the students to 'think for themselves', and learners may try hard to cloak their ignorance, or even their knowledge. (I know first-hand of one instance where a student pretended not to understand something because she felt that she had 'broken the rules' by reading on beyond where the teacher had directed.) What counts as knowledge may be arguable, in principle; but under normal classroom conditions, learners are unlikely to argue with a teacher's representations of 'the right answer'. We cannot avoid the issues of power and control in the construction of knowledge in classrooms, as a whole tradition of sociological and linguistic research has shown us.

Context and continuity

If a theory is going to explain how talk is used to create knowledge and understanding in the classroom, it must also incorporate two concepts. The first is *context*. 'Context' is not simply those things that exist around the talk, the physical objects and so on; it is those things beyond the words being spoken which contribute to the meaning of the talk. The things which are around in the setting are only contextual to the talk if the people who are talking use or respond to them in some way. What is more, the talk itself creates its own context; what we say at one time in a conversation creates the foundation for meanings in the talk which follows.[5] This is why, in Chapter 4, I described a conversation between a teacher and learner as one stretch of the road from the history of their relationship into its future.

The second, closely related concept that the theory must include is *continuity*. The process of creating knowledge in classrooms is one in which, for it to be successful, themes must emerge and continue, explanations must be offered, accepted and revisited, and understanding must be consolidated. Imagine that you are on a moving ship, watching a school of dolphins swim alongside. You may notice that they appear and disappear at irregular intervals. As you are watching, you notice a dolphin with a distinguishing mark appearing, disappearing and then reappearing above the surface. Sometimes that dolphin appears to drop out, though others continue to shadow the ship. You can follow the progress of the marked dolphin, even though it regularly disappears under the surface. The analyst of topics and themes in discourse has a similar experience; topics are introduced, discussed and then the conversation moves on. Some never surface again, but others do; when they do, this is because they are made to do so by the speakers.[6]

Creating context and continuity is natural for speakers, but that does not mean that they always do it well. If context and continuity are not well established in a conversation, the thread of a developing joint understanding may be broken and misunderstandings are likely to arise. In teaching and learning, this can create serious problems. This is illustrated by Sequence 3.6: *A simple rule for spelling*, on page 39. The teacher expected children to retain and use her 'simple rule', but their knowledge was not built upon firm foundations (see my comments following the sequence).

To illustrate the concept of continuity more clearly I would like you now to go back and look again at Sequence 2.5: *Key questions* on page 17. You will see again how the teacher 'sets up' the activity for the day by eliciting from the children some of the main teaching points from the previous lesson. The joint talk and action of the previous day provided a historical context for what was now unfolding. Then, look at the sequence below, from the same class but from the lesson after the one which provided Sequence 2.5. As it begins, the teacher has come along to help two boys who are having difficulties as they are trying to create a suitable 'key' for categorising sea-shells of various shapes and sizes.

Sequence 5.1: History in the making

Daniel: I can't think of a way to separate those two (*indicating two shells*). I've got to separate some of these.

Teacher: What's an obvious difference between them?

Daniel: They are cones.

Graham: They are pointed?

Teacher: All right. That would... (*long pause*) So you could separate those two but it wouldn't be a question that applies to those (*indicating two other shells*). Is there one difference between those two that is also a way you could group those?

Daniel: Well, that's pointed... (*indicates one shell*).

Teacher: um.

Daniel: ...and that one isn't.

[*And later, after the teacher has left...*]

Daniel: What was the last one we asked before this one?

Graham: 'Is it patterned?'

Daniel: No. Because these (*indicating shells*) are coiled and then we said...

Graham: 'Is it pointed?'

This conversation is not very easy for a reader to follow, because the speakers are drawing a lot on the objects, the shells, which form a necessary contextual part of their conversation. Without seeing the shells, we struggle to make sense of the meanings they are making together. But equally important to this meaning-making is the shared history of their earlier talk, as represented by Sequence 2.5. There is Daniel's slightly unusual, technical use of the word 'separate', echoed by the teacher. This carries even earlier echoes of Helen in Sequence 2.5, which in turn echoed its use by the teacher in other recordings not transcribed here. There is the standard format of their 'key questions' ('Is it patterned?', 'Is it pointed?') which again echoes the teacher's model question in earlier lessons. As the Russian literary theorist Bakhtin puts it, we learn words not from dictionaries but from people's mouths, and these words always carry with them some of the meanings of their earlier users.[7] In the classroom, this transfer of contextualised meaning is vital for students' learning. Notice, too, how in the last part of the sequence Daniel and Graham try to reconstruct the history of their own recent conversation — not all of it but the 'key questions' which are relevant to their current, educational interests and goals.

The 'long conversations' of teaching and learning

At a more general level, of course, the conversation in Sequence 5.1 builds a great deal of its meaning upon the earlier lesson (in Sequence 2.5). Imagine how much harder it would have been for you, as a reader, to make sense of Sequence 5.1 if you had not read the earlier sequence (and the information about the lesson that I provided). But it is difficult for me to demonstrate the importance of 'continuity' in this book, because it cannot easily be done by using short extracts from longer conversations. Even if I presented transcripts of whole lessons, these would still amount to extracts of a kind, because they are one of a series of related language events for the people involved. When a teacher and a group of learners are working together, the talk in one lesson can be thought of as one part of a 'long conversation' that lasts for the whole of their relationship.[8]

We all know from our own 'long conversations', with colleagues, friends, family and any other people that we meet repeatedly, that people talk about things that they and their listeners know happened in the past, and they also refer to things that they expect to happen in the future. Teachers sometimes do this in particularly obvious ways, even over quite short stretches of time (*recapping* and *elaborating* in the ways I described in Chapter 3) because they want students to see the connections between the things that they did 'last time', what they are doing now, and the goals that they are pursuing. I mentioned that we can see the teacher doing this at the beginning of Sequence 2.5. For another example, look back at Sequence 4.5: *'Perhaps'* on page 58. There we see the teacher explicitly recapping events which have only recently happened, because he wants to emphasise their significance for the children. And in Sequence 4.2: *Not a normal schoolday* on page 50, the teacher begins by summarising a history which both he and the student already know.

Of course, speakers are only as explicit as they feel is necessary. For example, look back at Sequence 3.2: *Dimensions*. The teacher and students are making lots of assumptions about each other's understanding about what is meant by 'rooms', who 'Cath' is, and so on, which would mean little to an outsider. Speakers can build heavily upon shared past experience but not make it explicit because some shared understanding can quite reasonably be taken for granted (this happens in written language too: later in this book I will assume that when I refer to 'long conversations', the words will echo this section). On the other hand, speakers may leave information implicit when one might, as a critical observer, have thought it would have been useful to bring it out into the open. Looking further on in the 'long conversation', we may find evidence that this did or did not cause problems.

Learning With Some Help

So far in this chapter I have briefly reviewed my own understanding of how language is used to create knowledge and understanding. I see it as a purposeful, persuasive process. People use language to pursue their interests and goals, to get things done. A theory of the guided construction of knowledge in classrooms has to do more than explain how people use talk to create knowledge as a joint, social possession. It also has to deal with the fact that one of the interests or goals that someone may be pursuing in a conversation is, quite self-consciously, to help someone else to learn. That is, the theory does not just have to deal with the ways that knowledge is shared as a matter of everyday events, but to take account of the fact that some people — teachers and learners — come together for the express purpose of one helping the other develop their knowledge and understanding. Here the ideas of two psychologists are particularly useful, L.S. Vygotsky (to whom I referred in Chapter 1) and Jerome Bruner (who was himself influenced by Vygotsky).[9] Working in the Soviet Union in the early part of the twentieth century, Vygotsky developed a theory of cognitive development which has only really become widely appreciated in the latter part of the century and sixty years after his death.[10] For most of the twentieth century, however, the most influential theorist of cognitive development has undoubtedly been Jean Piaget (whose theory strongly influenced the ideology of 'progressive' education).[11] Vygotsky's perspective on development differed from Piaget's in two main ways. First, he argued that language has a strong influence on the structure of thought. It is from him that I draw the idea of language as both an individual and a social mode of thinking. And secondly he emphasised that cognitive development is a social, communicative process. He drew attention to some features of human learning and development which are quite normal and commonplace, but which have too often been undervalued or ignored in psychology. One is that *learning with assistance or instruction is a normal, common and important feature of human mental development.* Another is that *the limits of a person's learning or problem-solving ability can be expanded if another person provides the right kind of cognitive support.*[12]

While Piaget saw his work as 'epistemology' (the study of the origins and nature of knowledge), Vygotsky's chosen field was 'pedagogy' (the study of the process of teaching and learning). From that perspective, he questioned some assumptions about children's intellectual development, assumptions which are still often made today by psychologists and teachers. One such assumption is that children's intellectual development is very much driven from within the individual, and that children's capacity for understanding is determined essentially by the 'cognitive level' that they have reached as individuals. Vygotsky, however, saw each developing child as someone whose achievements, at least in part, are determined by particular circumstances in which the learning takes place and by the contributions of other people involved. This does not mean that he thought that children do not differ in their innate capacity, or that if a learner 'fails' the responsibility lies entirely with the teacher rather than the learner. He meant that a learner's actual achievement is never just a reflection of that individual's inherent ability, but is also a measure of the effectiveness of the communication between a teacher and a learner.

Vygotsky invites us to consider how the conversations which take place in and around learning activities constrain or extend the intellectual potential of individual learners. A second assumption often made is that children learn best if they are given tasks which suit their level of development so that they can manage them without a teacher having to intervene. Piaget encouraged this by saying 'each time one prematurely teaches a child something he could have discovered for himself, the child is kept from inventing it and consequently from understanding it completely'.[13] Many educationalists have read his words as a warning for teachers to stay out, as much as possible, from the engagement of a child with a learning task. Vygotsky's view is rather different. He says 'Instruction is only good when it proceeds ahead of development',[14] and that the support of a teacher can enable learners to achieve levels of understanding that they never would alone. This implies that an activity which learners can do without any help is unlikely to be stretching their intellectual capabilities.

'Scaffolding' learning

So Vygotsky's theory, more than Piaget's, has room in it for teachers as well as learners. It draws our attention to the construction of knowledge as a joint achievement. Vygotsky provided us with a theory of the development of thought and language. His insights offer us a great deal that is relevant to understanding the relationship between a teacher and an individual learner, though he did not observe and explain how language is actually used to teach and to learn. However, Jerome Bruner has followed Vygotsky's line of interest and has studied the language of teaching and learning, mainly through observing young children interacting with their mothers. He uses the concept of 'scaffolding' to highlight the way that one person can become very intimately, and productively, involved in someone else's learning.[15] Bruner writes that:

> [Scaffolding] refers to the steps taken *to reduce the degrees of freedom* in carrying out some task so that the child can concentrate on the difficult skill she is in the process of acquiring.[16]

The concept is easy to relate to the experience of being a parent. For example, it is fairly common, in Europe anyway, to introduce children of about two years to jigsaw puzzles. At first, of course, they find the puzzles too hard, so a parent is likely to say something like 'Well, I'll do all the edges for you' and to assemble the 'frame' of the picture in front of the child's eyes. The child will next be encouraged to fill in the centre of the picture, with some help from the parent when required. In this way the impossible task facing the child is transformed into a manageable version. The process also allows the child to observe a successful strategy for doing the puzzle while making their own guided attempt. Over time, a parent can reduce how much help they give and encourage more active involvement on the part of the child (e.g. get them to hunt out all the 'edge' pieces) until the child can eventually do a jigsaw independently. Successful 'scaffolding' requires the adult to be sensitive to the child's competence in the task — responsibility is handed over to the extent that the child shows they are able to cope with it. For Bruner, 'scaffolding' describes a particular kind and quality of cognitive support which an adult can provide, through dialogue, so that a child can more easily make sense of a difficult task. He describes it as a form of 'vicarious consciousness' provided by the adult for the benefit of the child.

'Scaffolding' is an attractive concept for both psychology and education because it offers a neat metaphor for the active and sensitive involvement of a teacher in a student's learning. As well as being used by developmental psychologists studying parents and infants, it has been used in anthropological research into how craft skills (like weaving) are passed on from an expert to a novice, in situations where the expert is often more concerned with getting the job done than with teaching.[17] In the sense Bruner uses it, though, it represents something which seems like the essence of one kind of good teaching. There are of course other effective ways that people can be helped to learn, besides that of a teacher guiding a learner through an activity. People can sometimes learn very well through unguided exploration, and can also learn by listening passively to lectures or stories or by being directly instructed. But I am including the concept of 'scaffolding' in my sketch for a theory because it describes a quality of the process of teaching and learning which both 'progressive' and 'traditional' ideologies of education tend to ignore. It represents both teacher and learner as active participants in the construction of knowledge.

Given its attractiveness, it is not surprising that the term 'scaffolding' is now commonly used in educational research and by teachers discussing their own practice. However, I have some reservations about its being casually incorporated into the professional jargon of education, and applied loosely to various kinds of support teachers provide. The essence of the concept of scaffolding as used by Bruner is the sensitive, supportive intervention of a teacher in the progress of a learner who is actively involved in some specific task, but who is not quite able to manage the task alone. Any other kinds of help provided by teachers are better described as 'help'. There is also the danger that applying the concept in the classroom depends upon a simplistic comparison being made between what parents or craft experts do and what school teachers have to do (a comparison which Bruner's own use of 'scaffolding' has tended to encourage). But school-teachers and their students are operating under very different circumstances from parents and young children, or expert weavers and their apprentices. There is the obvious matter of teacher–learner ratios, and the more fragmented relationships which are inevitable in school. Also, some of the definitions of 'scaffolding' that have been used in studies of expert–apprenticeship learning and parental tutoring expressly include the criterion that *the 'expert' or 'tutor' is not self-consciously trying to teach, or is not primarily concerned with teaching* (being perhaps more concerned with simply entertaining a child in the case of parents, or with manufacture in the case of expert craft workers). This clearly does not describe the role of professional teacher.

A theory of the guided construction of knowledge in schools cannot be built upon comparisons with teaching and learning in other settings. To be useful, the concept of 'scaffolding' must be reinterpreted to fit the classroom.[18] One useful step would be to get away from the imagery of concrete, physical tasks like doing jigsaws or weaving cloth. Education is not about the physical manipulation of objects. A great deal of it is learning how to use language — to represent ideas, to interpret experiences, to formulate problems and to solve them. As I put it in Chapter 1, through conversations with parents, teachers, and other 'guides' we acquire ways of using language that can shape our thoughts. These ways of using language provide us with frames of reference with which we can 'recontextualise' our experiences. In schools, students are learning to take on new, educational frames of reference and apply these frames to interpret observations, information and events. 'Scaffolding' learning in school may be a matter of helping students to apply frames of reference that they only partially grasp and that they are inexperienced in applying. And it may be a process that involves more than two people. But a crucial, essential quality of 'scaffolding' in all settings must be that it is the provision of guidance and support which is increased or withdrawn in response to the developing competence of the learner.

Now look at the next sequence, recorded by a teacher in her own classroom in an English primary school. In it, she is helping a ten-year-old boy called Paul to master the method for doing subtractions known as 'decomposition' (so called because large numbers are broken down into smaller constituent numbers). The sum as they are doing it on paper is in the right-hand column. A second boy called Gary is also present, and as you will see he becomes involved in the teaching-and-learning.

Sequence 5.2: Subtraction using decomposition

Teacher:	OK right Paul, I'm going to give you a sum, right, and I want you to just tell me how you are doing it. OK this is the sum. You (*to Gary*) can do it as well and then I'll give you a different one — um — try and think of a nice…
Paul:	(*interrupting*) hard one
Teacher:	Hard one, OK.
Paul:	Oh no, oh no.
Teacher:	OK that's it (*writing*) and it's a subtraction.

$$\begin{array}{r} 133 \\ -69 \\ \hline \end{array}$$

Paul:	Oh no.
Teacher:	Now tell me what you actually do to start with. What do you say to yourself?
Paul:	Well, 3 minus 9 you can't do.
Teacher:	Yes.
Paul:	Cross that out and make that 2?
Teacher:	Yes.

$$\begin{array}{r} 1\overset{2}{\cancel{3}}3 \\ -69 \\ \hline 4 \end{array}$$

Paul:	So now you've got 13.
Teacher:	Correct.
Paul:	So that's 4.
Teacher:	Yes, correct.
Paul:	So that's 2 minus 6 you can't do so that's 1 take that's — down to zero.

$$\begin{array}{r} 0\,2 \\ \not1\not3'3 \\ 69 \\ \hline 4 \end{array}$$

Teacher:	Yes.
Paul:	And you get 120. Is that — is it 4 and 4?
Teacher:	Say that again, 120, what do you mean 120?
Paul:	Well (*loud noise occurs in background*).
Teacher:	That Mrs Hemington, she's so helpful, isn't she, with her stapler. Go on, say it again, just…
Paul:	Well, you've crossed that out (*indicating the '1' in the 'hundreds' column*).

Teacher:	Yes. What are you going to do with it, now you've crossed it out?
Paul:	Move it on to here (*indicating 'tens' column*).
Teacher:	Go on then. You haven't done that yet. I can't see it in there. It's vanished.
Paul:	So that's three.
Teacher:	Well, is it though?
Gary:	Hang on, put a one there, Paul.
Paul:	Right, OK.
Teacher:	What did you say Gary?
Gary:	Put a one.
Teacher:	What is that one? Where have you got that from?
Paul:	From the hundreds.
Teacher:	Right. So what number is that there now? (*indicating the 'tens' column*)

$$\begin{array}{r} 0\,12 \\ \not1\not3'3 \\ 69 \\ \hline 4 \end{array}$$

| Gary: | That is now 13. |
| Paul: | Um, what's that, oh, 12, oh (*makes choking noises*) sixty-four. |

$$\begin{array}{r} 0\,12 \\ \not1\not3'3 \\ 69 \\ \hline 64 \end{array}$$

| Teacher: | Is he right? |
| Gary: | Yes. |

This sequence shows the teacher doing something I would be happy to call 'scaffolding', as she leads Paul through the process of doing a subtraction. She encourages him to talk his way through the sequence of operations, to tell her what he is doing. By her prompts or elicitations ('What do you say to yourself?' 'what do you mean 120?') and confirmations ('Yes'/'Correct'), she 'steers' him through this particular problem-solving procedure. Her prompts, confirmations and queries ('Well, is it though?') provide a support for an activity in which the learner currently lacks competence and confidence. Paul is able to turn to her for confirmation of his actions (as in remarks like 'Cross that out and make that 2?'). His friend Gary also provides some help; but notice that it is a *different kind* of help, not 'scaffolding' but straightforward instruction about what to do next ('Hang on, put a one there, Paul'.). The teacher has, in the past, instructed members of the class on how to do subtractions, so those instructions are part of the history of the 'long conversation' about mathematics between her and Paul. At this stage, it seems, she wishes to avoid repeating direct instructions and to encourage Paul to act in a way which is, in relative terms, more independent. With the help of Gary and his teacher, Paul achieved what the developmental psychologists Tharp and Gallimore call an 'assisted performance'.[19] He then went on to do some subtractions successfully without any assistance. This therefore represented a complete sequence of 'scaffolded' learning, in which the teacher eventually withdrew her supportive guidance and the learner stood alone.

Making knowledge accountable

To some readers, it may seem strained and inappropriate for the teacher in Sequence 5.2 to require Paul to 'talk through' his actions. It might reasonably be objected that arithmetic need not be done through words, but through other kinds of mental imagery. What is more, people can be extremely adept at 'quick and dirty' mental strategies and yet lack the formal, more laborious procedures required in school. This, however, brings us to three points which are important for understanding educational knowledge and the way it is constructed in school. The first is an obvious point: the construction of knowledge requires that people put some things into words, even mathematical procedures which do not seem 'linguistic', simply so they can be shared. The second concerns one of the purposes of this sharing. The teacher needs to know what Paul is thinking so that she can assess his understanding and help him overcome his misunderstanding. One of her goals, presumably, is to eventually satisfy herself that Paul has achieved some independent mastery of this mathematical technique and an understanding of the principles involved.[20] The third point is more subtle, and really concerns the aims of education that I discussed earlier in the chapter — the ways of using language for 'framing' experience that students are meant to be acquiring in schools and other educational institutions. Students are expected not only to use these frames of reference for solving problems, they are expected to be *accountable* for the solutions they reach. [21] That is, their solutions are expected not only to be correct, but also *justifiable* in terms of mathematics, science, literary studies or whatever frame of reference applies. In her conversation with Paul, the teacher is eliciting this kind of *accountability* from him.

Later in the session with Paul, the teacher encouraged Gary (who was more able at maths) to describe to Paul how he would do these kinds of sums. After Gary had done so, she made the following comments:

Teacher: We need Paul to make sure he can do them. They're quite hard, aren't they? I think what you've done is explain what to do but without saying why. (*Another boy called Graham joins them.*) This time, Gary and Graham, we need to explain why we're doing what we're doing — there's no point in just saying 'cross that out, put that there'. It doesn't make sense unless there's a reason for it, because you won't remember it for next time, will you?

In her remarks to Gary and Graham, we can see here the teacher herself justifying — *accounting for* — her insistence on both procedures and principles being made explicit. Her argument is that 'a method doesn't make sense unless there's a reason for it', and that if he doesn't understand the reason he 'won't remember it for next time'. It might not be true, strictly speaking, that one cannot remember procedures without principles (I know many procedures on my word-processor that I could not explain in principle), but that is not the main point. The point is that the kind of mathematical understanding she wishes them to acquire is a deeper, principled understanding, not merely the ability to carry out an effective procedure, and it is this that she is arguing for. And she associates this kind of understanding with a certain way of expressing ideas and relationships — a particular form of educated discourse, the discourse of mathematics.

The Special Nature of Classroom Education

The third of my essential requirements for a theory of how talk is used to teach and learn was that it should incorporate some explanation of the special nature and purposes of formal education. By this, I meant that the theory must take into account the nature of schools and other educational institutions, as places where a special kind of learning is meant to happen.

Of course, as social institutions, schools have many purposes — to control children, to instil moral values, to train them in specific skills. They achieve a variety of effects, some of which may be intended (e.g. the empowerment of students) and others which may not be (e.g. the alienation and demoralisation of students — and teachers). A theory cannot deal with all these things, because if it did, it would not be a 'theory' any more, in the sense of a simplified explanatory model of one strand of real life; it would *be* real life in all its complexity. In any case, I am not trying to sketch a theory of educational practice, but only of part of it, the guided construction of knowledge. Yet the theory must still be a valid model, which can be seen to retain 'the important bits' of the life it models; and this is where I feel that contemporary psychology, even the socio-cultural kind, is weak. Although Vygotsky offers us valuable insights into the relationship between thought, language and culture, his theory was not based on research in classrooms. The more recent psychology of cognitive development has almost exclusively focused on the early years of life and is based on research carried out in laboratories, homes and day nurseries, not schools. I pointed out earlier that the concept of 'scaffolding' emerged from research on one-to-one relationships; parents and infants at home, expert craft workers with apprentices. At one level, the differences between these and classroom education are obvious — a matter of numbers of learners per teacher and their effects on the kind and quality of communications involved.[22] These are important in themselves. But one of the most crucial differences between classroom education and other, more informal kinds of teaching and learning is that in school there is a curriculum to be taught.

Discourse

The obvious and visible parts of a curriculum are the facts, the information, involved in the teaching and learning of particular subjects. But there is a more subtle quality to educational knowledge, which I raised in the discussion of how the concept of 'scaffolding' should be adapted to apply to classrooms. It is that one of the most important goals of education is to help students acquire, recognise and develop specific ways of using language. If we look outside psychology to linguistics, one concept which is useful here is *discourse*.[23] 'Discourse' in this sense means language as it is used to carry out the social and intellectual life of a community. In earlier chapters (particularly Chapter 3) I have shown how teachers in schools and other educational institutions use language in some typical and conventional ways as they go about their business. They involve students in Initiation–Response–Feedback (IRF) exchanges, they use the techniques of reformulation, repetition, cued elicitations and so on to try to guide the learning of their students. This is the discourse of teaching-and-learning in classrooms, which can be called *educational discourse*. But the important goal of education is not to get students to take part in the conventional exchanges of educational discourse, even if this is required of them on the way. It is to get students to develop new ways of using language to think and communicate, 'ways with words' which will enable them to become active members of wider communities of *educated discourse*.

One simplification I am making here, for the sake of my theory, is to describe 'educational' and 'educated' discourse as though they were separate entities. They are obviously interwoven. However, they are certainly not one and the same thing, and it is useful to distinguish them. I can demonstrate this distinction and explain why it is useful through some research by Eve Gregory, in an observational study of the teaching of reading in one British infant school classroom.[24] The teacher whom Gregory observed was one of many in British schools who have, in recent years, taken up the 'apprenticeship' model of teaching reading. In practice this means a planned move from a teacher-led reading of a book, through a phase where the teacher shares a book with children (or as in this case an individual child), until eventually each child can read the book alone. Reflecting the theory behind this approach, the teacher in question said that two of her aims were to *'model' the fluent reader* in her talk and behaviour and *to encourage the child to predict the story and the text*. I would like to paraphrase these aims as: *to show the child how a book is talked about in educated discourse*. However, the way the teacher talked to the various children did not have a simple and obvious relationship to these aims. With children who were 'making good progress' in reading (which Gregory based on the views of the teacher, the children and their and family), the teacher's talk with children could be seen to embody these aims. For example:

Teacher question: I wonder what might happen to the dog?

Child response: I don't know.

Teacher comment: *Turn over and we'll find out.*[25]

Here the teacher is responding positively to the child's interest in predicting what will happen in the story. She draws the child's attention to the way events are represented serially in the text; to find out what happens next, readers turn the page. Here is another example, with a child who was just beginning to learn English (but who was nevertheless considered to be making good progress as a reader of English):

Child:	What does that say?
Teacher:	*It says, 'Keep off...'*
Child:	'...the grass'. Why does it say 'Keep off the grass'?
Teacher:	Well, people aren't obviously supposed to walk on it, because if...
Child:	...so he's obviously stopped it from growing...
Teacher:	Mmm.
Child:	But he's going to walk off, isn't he?
Teacher:	*Yes. Shall we read on? It says...*[26]

Here the teacher draws the child's attention to the text, and the child responds appropriately by taking over the voice of the reader. This leads to some discussion about what is going on. Both teacher and child use what knowledge they have to make sense of what is meant to be happening in the text, after which the teacher suggests that they continue on the basis of this newly established joint understanding.

Gregory also noted that much of the talk between the 'good progress' readers and the teacher fitted the I–R–F exchange pattern of Initiation (by a teacher)–Response (by a child)–Feedback (by the teacher). The two examples above show this pattern. Through this familiar pattern of educational discourse, then, the teacher was not so much 'modelling' educated discourse for these children as 'scaffolding' it.[27]

However, when it came to the children who were 'having difficulties with reading', these kinds of exchanges — in terms of both their pattern and their content — were rare. Instead, the teacher provided children with far less 'feedback' on the comments they made, and she often allowed (or even encouraged) the conversation to swing away from the text into 'real life' topics. That is, the teacher did not use educational discourse in the same way, to scaffold children's entry into educated discourse — even though, paradoxically, in this group of children were the ones who would seem to need it most. Gregory suggests that one possible explanation for the teacher's behaviour with these two groups of children is the influence of 'child-centred' educational philosophy. Where the child seemed willing and able to use the book as the frame of reference for the conversation, the teacher was glad to encourage and support it. But when the child seemed unable or unwilling to do so, the teacher was reluctant to impose her frame of reference on the conversation.

Learners can only develop confidence in using new discourses by using them. Discourses are forms of language which are generated by the language practices of a group of people with shared interests and purposes.[28] While all students engage, as a matter of course, in *educational* discourse, they need opportunities to practise being users of *educated* discourse. One problem with most teacher-led discussions in the classroom is that they only offer students the opportunity to make brief responses — there is a mismatch between the educational discourse they are engaged in and the educated discourse they are meant to be entering. In the next chapter, I will consider ways that working together without a teacher can help learners make this kind of progress. But teachers can scaffold students' participation in educated discourse. Andy Northedge, the author of the popular and highly regarded *Good Study Guide*[29], has argued this very clearly in relation to discussion activity amongst first-year university students, but what he says is relevant to teaching students of all ages:

> Without a teacher a group discussion tends to gravitate towards a common denominator in terms of an 'everyday' discourse that everyone can understand and use effectively. Whereas, a teacher can, without necessarily dominating the discussion, help to translate some of what is said into terms of the 'academic' discourse, so that the group members can see how the ideas they already hold can be made to work within that discourse. The teacher can help to 'frame' the discussion by keeping some of the general purposes and styles of argument of the new discourse in play within the discussion, by posing questions, suggesting 'real-life' cases for discussion, probing arguments, asking for evidence and so on. In the context of a discussion it is not necessarily the teacher's role to 'explain' things (which would tend to cut across the dynamics of a collective 'discussion' — and a collectively-maintained consciousness). It is more to be the person who brings the language and the frames of reference of the 'expert' discourse into the 'collective consciousness' of the group.[30]

So Northedge is arguing that it is crucial that the language practices of the classroom (educational discourse) scaffold students' entry into educated discourse. He is also encouraging us to compare 'educated/academic discourse' with 'everyday discourse'.[31] I would combine this suggestion with ideas I have introduced earlier by suggesting that one important characteristic of educated discourse is that speakers must make their ideas *accountable* to specified bodies of knowledge and do so by following 'ground rules' which are different from those of most casual, everyday conversations. Of course, there is not just one educated discourse. For any academic subject or any occupational group, there are ways of using language which are not merely a matter of using the right 'local' technical terms. There are various ways of presenting information, telling stories or arguing cases (the 'genres' of English literature, scientific reports, business letters and so on) which are conventional in particular 'discourse communities'.[32] There are 'ground rules' for using language, solving problems and getting things done which have developed and which usually become taken for granted by members of each community. This certainly complicates life for teachers dealing with a whole curriculum of subjects (as in most primary schools), but it does not affect the basic argument which Northedge and others are making. One of the main aims of education is giving students access to discourses, even if one of its other important aims is the encouragement of innovation and creativity. People who make important creative contributions to any field of knowledge, even those who transcend the 'ground rules' and reshape the ideas of a community, can always 'speak the discourse'.

The teacher as discourse guide

I have stressed throughout this chapter that to be educationally relevant and useful, a theory of the guided construction of knowledge must take account of the social and institutional circumstances in which teachers and students communicate. As I mentioned earlier, one of the most obvious and crucial differences between teachers and most other 'guides to the construction of knowledge' (such as parents) is that teachers are responsible for the simultaneous advancement of large numbers of learners, and they have no opportunity to build intense, individualised relationships with them. They have to use *educational* discourse to organise, energise and maintain a local mini-community of *educated* discourse. We can think of each teacher as a *discourse guide* and each classroom as a *discourse village*, a small language outpost from which roads lead to larger communities of educated discourse. Think of the normal yearly course of events in schools and most other educational institutions. Each year, a new group of young people, some of whom may be complete strangers, enters a teacher's classroom. The students may share some past educational experience (depending on their age, and so on), but this may have been with other teachers and have dealt with some different topics. The teacher has the responsibility for building contextual foundations for the future learning of the students, and for creating continuity in the educational activities that the students engage in.

Teachers are expected to help their students develop ways of talking, writing and thinking which will enable them to travel on wider intellectual journeys, understanding and being understood by other members of wider communities of educational discourse: but the teachers have to start from where the learners are, to use what they already know, and help them go back and forth across the bridge from 'everyday discourse' into 'educated discourse'. Each teacher is working with a diverse group of learners who have arrived with their own histories, expectations and agendas (some of which will be in conflict with the teacher's agenda), and they can only communicate with these learners as a class, as groups or in brief individual conversations. In a primary school classroom, for example, the common patterns of communication are a teacher addressing a whole class, a teacher moving around a class and dipping into the activities of individuals, pairs and groups, and individual children making brief approaches to a teacher to get guidance or clarification on a specific matter. In these ways a teacher attempts to keep all the students within the collective enterprise of classroom discourse, and to make brief encounters part of a 'long conversation'. These features are not well handled by established theories of learning and cognitive development, which have all been designed to deal with fewer people doing the teaching and learning, and doing so in less complex social circumstances. The theory we need must recognise the essentially collective nature of classroom education, with its own aims and goals and with all its inherent diversity and conflict.

Summary and Conclusions

I began this chapter by justifying the need for a theory of how talk is used to guide the construction of knowledge. I suggested that the kind of theory which would be most helpful to both researchers and teachers would need to do three things. First, it must explain *how language is used to create joint knowledge and understanding*. Secondly, it must explain *how people help other people to learn*. And third, the theory must deal with *the special nature and purpose of formal education*. I have sketched a socio-cultural theory which might meet these requirements. According to the theory, talk is used to construct knowledge. This is a social, historical process, in the sense that the talk generates its own context and continuity, so that the knowledge that is created carries with it echoes of the conversations in which it was generated. It need not be a simple sharing, because knowledge can be created out of the conflict of ideas as much as through the accumulation and combination of them. People also use talk to pursue their own special aims and interests, and so conversations in which people are self-consciously trying to teach and to learn will have special characteristics. These characteristics reflect not only the functional pursuit of teaching and learning, but also the cultural histories of schools as social institutions and the accountabilities of teachers and students within them. The concept of 'scaffolding' is useful for describing how one person can become actively involved in another's learning activity, in such a way that the learner has an active role and yet is able to progress further and more easily than they could have done alone. However, the use of this concept must take into account the special nature of formal education, in which there is a curriculum to teach and where teachers are professionally responsible for teaching it. The curriculum does not consist simply of subject knowledge of a factual kind, but embodies ways of using language — discourses — which students need to be enabled to understand and to use if they are to become educated.

In most of the book so far, I have concentrated on how the construction of knowledge is guided by a teacher interacting with learners. In the next chapter, I will look instead at some ways that learners construct knowledge together, without the continuous presence of a teacher. I will develop some of the concepts and explanations I have offered in this chapter as I do so.

Notes

1 *Becoming Our Own Experts: Studies of Language and Learning made by the Talk Workshop Group at Vauxhall Manor School, 1974–1979.* London: Talk Workshop Group, 1982, p 1.

2 'I'm trying to get rid of the 1960s theorist': British Secretary of State for Education Mr Kenneth Clarke, on BBC Radio 4, 15 Dec 1991. See also Clarke, K. (1991) *Primary Education — A Statement by the Secretary of State for Education and Science.* London: DES. For the reassertion of the 'traditionalist' perspective see O'Hear, A. (1987) The importance of traditional learning. *British Journal of Educational Studies* 35 (2), pp. 102–14; Scruton, R. (1987) Expressionist education. *Oxford Review of Education* 13 (1), pp. 39–44; and for a redefinition of the 'progressive' stance, see Silcock, P. (1993) Towards a new progressivism in primary school education. *Educational Studies* 19 (1), pp. 107–21.

3 The concept of 'moral panic' comes from Cohen, S. (1973) *Folk Devils and Moral Panics: The Creation of Mods and Rockers.* London: Paladin.

4 See, for example, Drew, P. and Heritage, J. (1992) (eds) *Talk at Work: Interaction in Institutional Settings.* Cambridge: Cambridge University Press.

5 See Edwards, D. and Mercer, N. (1987) *Common Knowledge* (Chapters 3, 6 and 7). London: Methuen/Routledge. Also Mercer, N. (1992) Culture, context and the construction of knowledge in the classroom. In P. Light and G. Butterworth (eds) *Context and Cognition: Ways of Learning and Knowing.* Hemel Hempstead: Harvester-Wheatsheaf; and Coll, C. and Onrubia, J. (1994) Temporal dimensions and interactive processes in teaching-learning activities: A theoretical and methodological challenge. In N. Mercer and C. Coll (eds) *Explorations in Socio-cultural Studies, Vol. 3: Teaching, Learning and Interaction.* Madrid: Infancia y Aprendizaje.

6 See Edwards and Mercer (note 5).

7 Bakhtin, M. (1986) *Speech Genres and Other Late Essays* (ed. Caryl Emerson and Michael Holquist). Austin: University of Texas Press; also see Maybin, J. (1994) Children's voices: Talk, knowledge and identity. In D. Graddol, J. Maybin and B. Stierer (eds) *Researching Language and Literacy in Social Context.* Clevedon: Multilingual Matters.

8 This very useful notion of the 'long conversation' comes from Janet Maybin.

Maybin, J. (1994) Children's voices: Talk, knowledge and identity. In D. Graddol, J. Maybin and B. Stierer (eds) *Researching Language and Literacy in Social Context* (p. 136). Clevedon: Multilingual Matters.

9   Vygotsky's own work is well represented by Vygotsky, L.S. (1978) *Mind in Society*. London: Harvard University Press; and Bruner's by Bruner, J.S. (1986) *Actual Minds, Possible Worlds*. London: Harvard University Press; and (1990) *Acts of Meaning*. London: Harvard University Press.

10 For example Piaget, J. (1970) *The Science of Education and the Psychology of the Child*. New York: Viking Press. See also Sutherland, P. (1992) *Cognitive Development Today: Piaget and his Critics*. London: Paul Chapman.

11 A short, introductory discussion of the impact and educational relevance of Vygotsky's work can be found in Mercer, N. (1994a) Neo-Vygotskian theory and education. In B. Stierer and J. Maybin (eds) *Language, Literacy and Learning in Educational Practice*. Clevedon: Multilingual Matters. That book also includes extracts from Vygotsky's own writing and an article by Bruner. For fuller discussions, see Wertsch, J.V. (1985) (ed.) *Culture, Communication and Cognition: Vygotskian Perspectives*. Cambridge: Cambridge University Press; and Moll, L. (1990) (ed.) *Vygotsky and Education: Instructional Implications and Applications of Socio-historical Psychology*. Cambridge: Cambridge University Press.

12 Vygotsky's dynamic and social conception of an individual's intellectual capability is summed up in his concept of the Zone of Proximal Development (ZPD), which I take to represent the difference between what a learner can achieve alone and what they can achieve with 'scaffolding' support. See Cole, M. (1985) The Zone of Proximal Development: Where culture and cognition create each other. In Wertsch, J.V. (1985) (ed.) *Culture, Communication and Cognition: Vygotskian Perspectives*. Cambridge: Cambridge University Press; and Rogoff, B. and Wertsch, J. (1984) Children's learning in the Zone of Proximal Development. In W. Damon (ed.) *New Directions in Child Development No.23*. San Francisco: Jossey Bass.

13 Piaget, J. (1970) Piaget's theory. In P.H. Mussen (ed.) *Carmichael's Manual of Child Psychology* (p. 715). New York: Wiley.

14 Vygotsky, L.S. (1934), cited in Wertsch, J.V. (1985) *Vygotsky and the Social Formation of Mind* (p. 71). Cambridge, MA: Harvard University Press.

15 Wood, D., Bruner, J. and Ross, G. (1976) The role of tutoring in problem-solving. *Journal of Child Psychology and Child Psychiatry*, 17, 89–100.

16 This definition comes from Bruner, J.S.(1978) The role of dialogue in language acquisition. In A. Sinclair, R. Jarvella and W. Levelt (eds) *The Child's Conception of Language* (p.19). NewYork: Springer-Verlag. See also Wood, D. (1988) *How Children Think and Learn*. Oxford: Basil Blackwell.

17 Greenfield, P.M. (1984) A theory of the teacher in the learning activities of everyday life. In B. Rogoff and J. Lave (eds) *Everyday Cognition: Its Development in Social Context*. Cambridge, MA: Harvard University Press. Greenfield usefully identifies six features of 'scaffolded learning' which are common to both parentally-assisted language acquisition and learning to weave; but one of these (which distinguishes both kinds of events from those in school) is that the teacher is generally unaware of her teaching function.

18 Brown and Palincsar have made an operational definition of scaffolding in terms of specific techniques used by teachers, but this was done as part of their experimental training programme on 'reciprocal teaching' rather than for the

analysis of observational data. See Palincsar, A.M. (1986) The role of dialogue in providing scaffolded instruction. *Educational Psychologist* 21 (1&2), pp. 73–98. For other attempts to operationally define scaffolding in the everyday life of the classroom, see Maybin, J., Mercer, N. and Stierer, B. (1992) 'Scaffolding' learning in the classroom. In K. Norman (ed.) *Thinking Voices*. London: Hodder & Stoughton; Mercer, N. and Fisher, E. (1993) How do teachers help children to learn? An analysis of teachers' interventions in computer-based activities. *Learning and Instruction* 2, pp. 339–55.

19 Tharp, R. and Gallimore, R. (1990) A theory of teaching as assisted performance. In P. Light, S. Sheldon and M. Woodhead (eds) *Learning to Think: Child Development in Social Context* 2 (p. 58). London: Routledge. Barbara Rogoff's concept of 'guided participation' is a broader, more flexible notion than 'assisted performance', and it (like 'scaffolding') can perhaps be adapted to apply to school experiences. However, both these concepts are derived from the study of mother–child dyads, and are only applied by analogy to classrooms (see Rogoff, B. (1990) *Apprenticeship in Thinking: Cognitive Development in Social Context* (p. 8). New York: Oxford University Press.

20 'The gradual release of responsibility' is the expression used by Pearson (1985) in describing how teachers can wean students away from teacher dependence. Pearson, P. (1985) Changing the face of reading comprehension instruction. *The Reading Teacher* 38 (8), 724–38. See also Rodrigues Rojo, R. (1994) Book reading in classroom interaction: From dialogue to monologue. In N. Mercer and C. Coll (eds) *Explorations in Socio-cultural Studies, Vol. 3: Teaching, Learning and Interaction*. Madrid: Infancia y Aprendizaje.

21 This use of 'frames of reference' is taken from Barnes, D. and Todd, F. (1977) *Communication and Learning in Small Groups*. London: Routledge & Kegan Paul.

22 As Caroline Gipps points out, in a review of the relevance of research to primary school practice, all teaching would be probably easier in smaller classes but the reality of life for most teachers the world over is large classes with even larger ones to come. See Gipps, C. (1994) What we know about effective primary teaching. In J. Bourne (ed.) *Thinking Through Primary Practice*. London: Routledge.

23 See Chapter 2, 'The concept of discourse community', in Swales, J. (1990) *Genre Analysis: English in Academic and Research Settings*. Cambridge: Cambridge University Press. The concept of a 'community of discourse' is an attractive one, though (like the concept of 'scaffolding') it is often used very loosely. Swales uses it to describe a group of individuals who have some agreed common goals, some established networks of communication, and some distinctive terminology and ways of using language (which he calls 'genres'). Individual members of the community may come and go, but the community and its discourse transcend these changes. Amongst other things, membership depends on being able to 'speak' the discourse. See also Sheeran, Y. and Barnes, D. (1992) Oracy and genre. In K. Norman (ed.) *Thinking Voices*. London: Hodder & Stoughton.

24 Gregory, E. (1993) What counts as reading in the early years' classroom? *British Journal of Educational Psychology* 63, pp. 214–30. For a socio-cultural approach to reading in the classroom, see also Bloome, D. (1993) Necessary indeterminacy and the microethnographic study of reading as a social process. *Journal of Research in Reading* 16 (2), pp. 98–111.

25 Gregory (1993, note 24) p. 220 (italics as original).

26 Gregory (1993, note 24) p. 220.
27 But see Ellis and Rogoff's research, which suggests that students see the IRF patterns of educational discourse primarily as means of assessment rather than teacher co-operative support. Ellis, S. and Rogoff, B. (1986) Problem-solving in children's management of instruction. In E. Mueller and C. Cooper (eds) *Process and Outcome in Peer Relationhips*. San Diego: Academic Press.
28 See Swales (1990, note 23).
29 Northedge, A. (1990) *The Good Study Guide*. Milton Keynes: The Open University.
30 Northedge, A. (in press) *Making Sense of Studying*. London: Macmillan.
31 Vygotsky made a similar comparison between 'scientific' and 'everyday' language and concepts: Vygotsky, L.S., Thinking and Speech. In R. Rieber and A. Carton (1987) (eds) *The Collected Works of L.S. Vygotsky, Vol.1: Problems of General Psychology*. New York: Plenum.
32 See Lemke, J.L. (1990) *Talking Science: Language Learning and Values*. Norwood, NJ: Ablex; also Wells, G. (1994) The complementary contributions of Halliday and Vygotsky to a language-based theory of learning. *Linguistics and Education* 6 (1), 41–90.

6 Talking and Working Together

Introduction

So far in this book, I have mainly been looking at conversations between teachers and learners. Except for a few examples, I have not given much attention to how knowledge and understanding can develop when learners talk and work together without a teacher. Yet 'collaborative learning', as it is usually called, is important in our everyday lives. Think back through your own life: you will probably find, as I do, that a lot of knowledge and many valuable skills have been acquired through talking and working with people who were not, in any formal sense, your teachers. And this may not simply be a matter of being helped to learn by a more able friend: I know that on some occasions my own understanding has improved through having to explain something to a friend who understood it *less* well and asked for help. One good test of whether or not you really understand something is having to explain it to someone else. And an excellent method for evaluating and revising your understanding is arguing, in a reasonable manner, with someone whom you can treat as a social and intellectual equal.

However, the history of educational practice shows that talk amongst students has rarely been incorporated into the process of classroom education. Traditionally, talk between learners in the classroom has been discouraged and treated as disruptive and subversive. Although ideas may have changed to some extent in recent years, pupil–pupil talk is still regarded suspiciously by many teachers. As any teacher will confirm, one way that they feel that their competence is judged by senior staff, pupils, parents, and the rest of the world is: can they keep their classes quiet? [1] Of course, the reasonable explanation for the traditional discouragement of pupil–pupil talk is that, as an incidental accompaniment to whole-class, chalk-and-talk teaching, it is disruptive and subversive. Even in less formal regimes, teachers have an understandable concern with limiting the amount of 'off-task' talk that goes on. So while the experience of everyday life supports the value of collaborative learning, educational practice has implicitly argued against it. Is there evidence from research which can tell us more about the value of collaborative talk and activity?

Research on Collaboration in Learning

Communication between learners has not figured prominently in theories of the development of knowledge and understanding. Piaget, in his early work, sketched out a role for the significance of interaction between peers — it helped children to 'decentre', to become sensitive to other perspectives on the world than their own.[2] In his later work, with its focus on the activities of individuals, he did not give the topic much attention. But there have been some interesting recent developments in the Piagetian tradition. Followers of Piaget such as Willem Doise, Anne-Nelly Perret-Clermont and Gabriel Mugny have used the concept of *socio-cognitive conflict* to take account of how a child's understanding may be shifted by interacting with another child who has a rather different understanding of events.[3] The basic idea is that when two contrasting world-views are brought into contact, and the resulting conflict has to be resolved to solve a problem, this is likely to stimulate some 'cognitive restructuring' — some learning and improved understanding. The concept of socio-cognitive conflict has some interesting potential for the study of joint activity in the classroom. For example, it might be useful for explaining the kind of learning experience that took place in Sequence 2.3 *Maximum Box* (Chapter 2). But neo-Piagetians have not studied the actual talk involved in such conflicts of ideas — perhaps because, as I suggested in Chapter 5, language still occupies a relatively marginal role in their theory. The main aim in most of their research has also been to determine whether interaction improved later *individual* performance (rather than being interested in the construction of knowledge as a shared entity).

Vygotsky's theory, on the other hand, is essentially concerned with teaching-and-learning, rather than joint learning. Some of his neo-Vygotskian followers have researched learners' joint activity, but unlike the Piagetians they have tended to stress co-operation rather than conflict.[4] Most of this research involves adapting ideas from the study of 'asymmetrical' (i.e. teacher–learner) relationships to the study of more symmetrical ones (i.e. learner–learner). Thus Bruner[5] talks of how a 'more competent peer' can provide the scaffolding support for a learner, but this leaves an interesting question unanswered: what if peers are not more competent? Others have since suggested that having to explain your own ideas to someone you are learning with, whatever their relative ability, is useful because it encourages the development of a more explicit, organised, 'distanced' kind of understanding.[6] But we still lack suitable concepts for dealing with this process.

Although theory may not have kept pace, there has been a great deal of research interest in collaborative learning in recent years. Collaborative activity has been researched in various ways — through large-scale surveys of life in many classrooms, experiments in which pairs or groups carry out specially-designed problem-solving tasks, and detailed analyses of the talk of pairs or groups of children working together on curriculum-based tasks in school. One of the strengths of recent research on talk and learning, in fact, is that it has been so multidisciplinary and diverse in its methods. I will briefly review each of these lines of enquiry, and try to draw out the main points which are relevant here.

Surveys of classroom activity

Although it is certainly true that talk amongst pupils has tended to be discouraged in schools, at some times and in some places communication and interaction between children in the classroom has been officially sanctioned. Since the 1960s, a 'progressive' philosophy of education has encouraged 'group work' in British primary schools, in which children sit together around tables and are allowed to talk (at least to a limited extent) as they work. It is surprising, then, that little was known about the quality of most of this group work until the 1980s, when a large-scale research project called ORACLE[7] observed and evaluated practice in a large number of British primary schools. Did this provide evidence of the value of talk and joint activity for children's educational progress? The brief answer is 'no'. To be more precise, ORACLE did not show that collaborative activity was not valuable, it showed that it rarely happened. In most of the primary classrooms the researchers observed, the fact that children were sitting together at a table did not mean that they were collaborating. Usually, children at any table would simply be working, in parallel, on individual tasks. While they might well talk as they worked, and while they might possibly talk to each other about their work, the activities they were engaged in did not encourage or require them to collaborate or to talk about their work. ORACLE's surprising conclusion, then, was that most British primary classrooms were not good testing grounds for the value of collaborative learning and talk.

Since then, further research by members of the ORACLE team and others has provided mixed support for the value of group-based learning activities in classrooms. One clear implication of these findings is that we should not assume that group-based learning is inevitably valuable — it depends on what purpose it has, and how it is organised by the teacher. In their review of studies of group work in primary classrooms (and some experimental studies) Galton and Williamson conclude: 'For successful collaboration to take place, pupils need to be taught how to collaborate so that they have a clear idea of what is expected of them'.[8] This is very relevant to our interests here, so far as it goes. However, little of the research reviewed by Galton and Williamson included any close analysis of pupils' talk.

In the late 1980s, the National Oracy Project provided a wealth of information about talk in British schools, including such under-researched topics as children's own conceptions of how talk helps learning. It also succeeded in demonstrating the relevance of understanding the role of talk in learning for teachers of all curriculum subjects (not just English).[9] This was not done through surveys, but rather through the gathering of 'case studies' of classroom observations and practice, usually written by teachers themselves. In its early stages it provided some revealing information about what children think their teachers think about the value of talk in the classroom — that 'talk stops you working', 'talking is not work' and 'if you are allowed to talk, the work is not important'. I was closely involved with the National Oracy Project, and it seems to me that one of its main achievements was to raise teachers' awareness of the potential value of talk, and so improve the status of classroom talk amongst both teachers and pupils.

Experimental research

In Europe and the USA in recent years there have been many experimental comparisons of children working in pairs or groups. Typically this research has focused on outcomes — for example, do children achieve better results when working competitively or co-operatively? — and also usually on individual learning outcomes (rather than the process of learning together). Some of the findings of this research support the value of collaborative learning: but others have shown how under some conditions working with a partner is less effective than working on your own. Some experiments have been designed to determine what makes the crucial difference. One factor that does seem important is whether or not the experimental conditions are such that the children have to communicate and collaborate to solve a problem (rather than simply being allowed to do so).[10] On the basis of studying children working in pairs (without teacher support) on computer-based problems, the psychologist Paul Light suggests that having to use language to make plans explicit, to make decisions and to interpret feedback seems to facilitate problem-solving and promote understanding. One of the tasks used by Light and his fellow researchers was a kind of adventure game, in which the quest was to find and rescue a king's crown, hidden on an island (shown on a map on the computer screen). Choosing from a range of possible strategies, the children could manipulate several characters and means of transport to avoid the pirates who blocked their way. The analysis of children's talk showed that those pairs who did most verbal planning, negotiation and discussion of feedback were the most successful in solving the problems.[11] Using talk to reconcile conflicting suggestions for action seemed particularly important, and successful pairs also seemed to be those in which decision-making was most evenly shared between partners. Under such conditions, both children of a pair often learned better than when working alone. On the other hand, this research does not support the idea that working with 'a more competent peer' (as Jerome Bruner put it) is necessarily helpful for learning, as children who were considered to be of similar ability seemed to learn better than those in more asymmetrical pairs. Working with a more knowledgeable and capable partner who dominates decision-making and insists on the use of their own problem-solving strategies may hinder rather than help the less able.[12]

There has also been some recent interest in how collaborative activity affects the quality of thinking. For example, some experimental research has considered whether discussion helps children to *generalise* what they have learned (by 'generalise', I mean the extent to which they are able to use what they have learned in one situation, through solving one specific kind of problem, to deal with other related situations and problems). This interest arose because previous research had shown that, as a rule, children do not find it easy to generalise their understanding from one kind of problem or one area of the curriculum to another.[13] To some extent, this seems to be because their understanding is often 'procedural' rather than 'principled' — they learn to follow some practical procedures (e.g. learning a particular method for doing long divisions, or for doing science experiments and writing them up) without ever coming to understand the underlying principles involved.[14] There is now support for the idea that through sharing ideas, children can achieve more generalisable kinds of understanding if they are actively helped and encouraged to do so. For example, George Hatano and Kayoko Inagaki investigated how well some Japanese six-year-olds could use their experience of raising one kind of pet animal (e.g. a goldfish) to make sense of the life processes and care needs of other living things. One of their conclusions, which is particular relevant here, is that when children had to share ideas about caring for animals —

to explain, discuss and sometimes justify the opinions they held — this led to a better, more generalisable and 'principled' understanding.[15]

Research on talk between pupils in the classroom

Experiments can be useful for identifying which factors in the complex reality of joint learning and problem-solving seem more important for success than others. But it is difficult to draw implications for educational practice from experiments which were carried out under controlled conditions away from the normal life of classrooms and on tasks which are unrelated to the content of school curricula. Moreover, the great majority of experiments have been concerned with the outcomes of joint activity, and not the process itself. It is therefore interesting to look at the findings of a different style of research altogether, one which has concentrated on the process of discussion in classrooms rather than on its outcomes, and see whether it leads to similar or different conclusions. Two pioneers of this kind of research were Douglas Barnes and Frankie Todd, whose research in the 1970s is described in their classic book *Discussion and Learning in Small Groups*.[16] They showed how knowledge can be treated by pupils or students as a *negotiable* commodity when they are enthusiastically engaged in joint tasks. They suggest that pupils are more likely to engage in open, extended discussion and argument when they are talking with peers outside the visible control of their teacher, and that this kind of talk enables them to take a more active and independent 'ownership' of knowledge. As Barnes and Todd put it:

> Our point is that to place the responsibility in the learners' hands changes the nature of that learning by requiring them to negotiate their own criteria of relevance and truth. If schooling is to prepare young people for responsible adult life, such learning has an important place in the repertoire of social relationships which teachers have at their disposal.[17]

Barnes and Todd provide some examples of talk being used to good effect to construct knowledge and understanding, and in ways that are educationally appropriate. A good example is where, after a discussion of a topic, one of the group *summarises* what has emerged from the various contributions speakers have made. The next sequence is from their book. A group of 13-year-olds were discussing Steinbeck's novel *The Pearl*, and various members had commented on episodes in the book which they found unconvincing. After one such comment (the one by Barbara, below), Marianne offered a summary as follows:

Barbara: (*Returning to previous sub-topic*) I think he should describe more, you know. It's supposed to be about diving and pearls.

Marianne: (*Summarising consensus already attained*) Yeah we don't think we don't think there's adequate description.[18]

This kind of summary *recap* and *reformulation* is often made by teachers who are leading a class discussion (see Sequence 3.3 in Chapter 3, and my comments which follow it). It is not a common feature of 'everyday discourse', but it is an important feature of both 'educational' and 'educated discourse'. Perhaps Marianne was taking as her model for educated discourse her teachers' past contributions to educational discourse. Barnes and Todd also show how some group discussions seemed to achieve nothing at all, in educational terms. In the following example, a group of girls are discussing 'Gang violence' and using their own experience to explain why boys fight each other. (Note: brackets show simultaneous speech.)

Elizabeth: It wasn't an argument, he din't even er, anyhow, why do you think boys fight in gangs like this?... Yes, Shirley.

Shirley: I wasn't saying nothing.

Elizabeth: [My mother says that...

Catherine: [It's, it's, it's like a match in't it?

Shirley: Yeah.

Elizabeth: Yeah it is...

Catherine: Mind you it's impossible to change now, isn't it?

Shirley: Yeah.

Elizabeth: Chains

Catherine: [Mind you

Elizabeth: [Chains

Catherine: If them people didn't watch the programmes that they put on, some of 'em wouldn't do it.

Elizabeth: Yeah that's it they get most of the violence off the telly.[19]

And so the girls continued, say Barnes and Todd, at great length. They comment: 'What we see going on here is not the use of talk to construct new meanings but a set of unexamined platitudes which are never made quite explicit. If they had been made more explicitly, they would have been more available to criticism and modification. The girls do not advance their understanding in this extract; they merely reiterate half-understandings which they already possess'.[20]

Barnes and Todd are suggesting that classroom discussion has to meet certain requirements for explicitness which would not normally be required in 'everyday' discourse. Relevant information should be shared

effectively, opinions should be clearly explained and explanations examined critically: that knowledge should, as I put it in Chapter 5, be made
publicly *accountable*. Whatever value the talk might have had for consoli-
dating the girls' friendship, or commiserating about the failings of their
male companions, there is no reason to believe that this discussion was
helping them to advance their analytical understanding of issues in a way
that was *educationally* appropriate. Barnes and Todd argue that the
successful pursuit of educational activity through group work depends on
learners (a) sharing the same ideas about what is relevant to the discussion;
and (b) having a joint conception of what is trying to be achieved by it. These
points have been supported by other subsequent research.[21]

Social relationships

I made the point in Chapter 4 that education never takes place in a social
or cultural vacuum. Although schools are places with their own special
kinds of knowledge and their own ways of using language, and their own
power relationships, they do not stand outside the wider society. And
learners have social identities which affect how they act, and how other
people act, in the classroom. At one level, this point may be glaringly
obvious to teachers, who are every day made aware of the diversity of their
students. It is more easily forgotten by researchers whose tunnel vision
locks them into the study of certain aspects of intellectual development and
learning (I speak here from my experience as both a teacher and a
researcher). However, many researchers are now realising that social and
cultural factors must be given more attention[22]; and as the research by
Biggs and Edwards (described in Chapter 4) illustrated, even teachers may
be unaware of quite how such factors affect what goes on in their
classrooms. There has not yet been a great deal of research on the effects of
social and cultural factors on collaboration in the classroom, but there are
some findings which are very relevant to both research and practice.

Gender relations is one topic that has, in recent years, been studied by
both experimental and observational researchers. For instance, Joan Swann
has shown very clearly how the different interactive styles of boys and girls
can influence the ways knowledge is constructed, and so affect the quality
of the learning experience for those involved.[23] Although there is a lot of
individual variation amongst males and females, male students of all ages
tend to dominate discussions, to make more direct and directive comments
to their partners, and generally tend to adopt more 'executive' roles in joint
problem-solving. These kinds of differences are perhaps now well appreciated, at least in general terms, by teachers and researchers; the problem

is, as Swann says, knowing what to do about them.[24] However, she also highlights some 'blind spots' in the ways collaborative talk is evaluated, and her argument carries clear messages for researchers and teachers. A good illustration is her analysis of some video-taped examples of collaborative activity produced by a local education authority for the training of teachers, which compared children working in different girl–boy pairs.[25] On the video, 'successful' and 'unsuccessful' collaborations were illustrated by pairs building model cranes together from Lego, with 'success' apparently being measured by the design quality and sturdiness of the crane they made. But Swann points out that the 'success' of one pair was only achieved by a girl submitting to her male partner's verbal bossiness and accepting the role of his 'assistant'. In this role she had little influence on the design, her views were not taken seriously and a lot of the talk consisted of him giving her instructions. Swann points out that the collaboration and interaction were only being evaluated in terms of *outcome* (i.e. how well the crane was constructed), not *process*, with the result that some important aspects of the quality of educational experience for the children involved were being ignored.

Research has shown that while boys often dominate mixed-sex pair and group activity, sometimes the 'more able' students (of either sex) seem to be those who tend to take control.[26] All such findings draw our attention to the need for teachers and researchers to be clear about what criteria they are using to evaluate collaborative activity. The basic question is: 'what are the students expected to get from it?' If one reason for encouraging joint activity is so that all students get the opportunity to use language actively to solve problems, and another is to free them from the constraints of teacher-led discourse, it is hardly satisfactory if some students are often still trapped in reactive roles and have to contend with a different form of dominance.

A rather different aspect of social relations is the effect of friendship on the quality of discussion. Research in this fairly new field is well illustrated by an experiment by Margarita Azmitia and Ryan Montgomery, who set pairs of 11-year-olds some problems that required logical, scientific reasoning (one was a Sherlock Holmes type of mystery, involving death from a poisoned pizza). They found that when children were paired with friends rather than mere acquaintances, they did more explicit, 'scientific' reasoning through language and so solved the problems more successfully.[27]

What kind of talk should be encouraged, and how?

The research I have reviewed does not provide a neat set of findings which can easily be integrated or reconciled. But my review leads me to the conclusion that talk between learners has been shown to be valuable for the construction of knowledge. Joint activity provides opportunities for practising and developing ways of *reasoning with language*, and the same kinds of opportunities do not arise in teacher-led discourse. This conclusion can be used to justify 'group work' and other forms of collaborative activity in the classroom. But the research also shows that while encouraging talk between learners may help the development of understanding, not all kinds of talk and collaboration are of equal educational value.

It is possible to distil from the findings of research a description of a kind of talk which is good for solving intellectual problems and advancing understanding. First, it is talk in which partners present ideas as clearly and as explicitly as necessary for them to become shared and jointly evaluated. Second, it is talk in which partners *reason* together — problems are jointly analysed, possible explanations are compared, joint decisions are reached. From an observer's point of view, their reasoning is *visible* in the talk.

The research also helps us describe some favourable *conditions* for the emergence of this kind of talk. First, partners must *have* to talk to do the task, so their conversation is not merely an incidental accompaniment. Second, the activity should be designed to encourage co-operation, rather than competition, between partners. Third, participants must have a good, shared understanding of the point and purpose of the activity. And fourth, the 'ground rules' for the activity should encourage a free exchange of relevant ideas and the active participation of all involved. It also helps, as one might expect, if partners have an established, friendly relationship. There are some messages for both teachers and researchers in this list, which I will take up later in the chapter.

Back to the Classroom

I want now to look at some examples of children talking together in classrooms. The three sequences which follow were all recorded in a school in which I was researching as part of the SLANT (Spoken Language and New Technology) project.[28] Overall, we recorded approximately 50 hours of classroom talk in ten English primary schools. Our main interests in the project were to see how computer-based activities stimulated talk amongst children, and to understand the role of the teacher in organising and supporting joint activity at the computer. Other publications by the SLANT team deal with computer-related matters; but here I want to use the SLANT recordings to illustrate some general features of the quality of talk of children working together and the teacher's role in supporting it. The three sequences I have selected come from sessions which varied in length from about 35 to 90 minutes, reflecting differences in the kinds of activities that the children were engaged in. The sessions that provided these sequences were recorded over a period of 14 months in the same school — a modern primary with a mixed catchment on a city housing estate. The children in them were all aged 9–10 years, and came from the same locality. Each of the pairs or groups involved were recorded working in sets of related sessions, spread over days or weeks, and researchers also spent some time talking to both the teachers and the children. In all three sequences, the children can be observed to be solving some kind of problem and talking as they do so. And in all of them, the children can be seen to be well 'on task', in that they are dealing enthusiastically with legitimate aspects of the work they have been set by their teacher.

I have much more information about each of these sequences than I can easily share with you here. But on the basis of the limited information I can provide, I would like you, the reader, to do the following activity. First of all read through all three sequences. Look at the background information that I give before each one, but *ignore* for now the comments that I make later, after the final sequence. Drawing on what I have said earlier in the book, and especially in this chapter so far, consider the following questions for each sequence in turn:

(1) Do the children disagree at all?

(2) Do they ask each other questions?

(3) Do they share knowledge which is relevant to the task?

(4) Do they seem to have a common understanding of what the task is about?

(5) How well does the discussion seem to embody the kind of 'ground rules' for reasoning and problem-solving that are important for educational success?

After doing this, read the later comments I make and compare your analysis with mine.

In the first sequence, two ten-year-old boys, Sean and Lester, are using the program Smile,[29] which provides a series of mathematics-related puzzles. The puzzle that they are doing involves finding an elephant lost in New York (its streets being represented by a grid on the screen) by keying in co-ordinates and reacting to computer feedback on how close they get to their hidden target. Following their teacher's instructions, they take consecutive turns to key in pairs of co-ordinates. They have been doing the puzzle for about five minutes.

Sequence 6.1: Finding the elephant

Lester:	1, 2, 3, 4, 5 (*counting grid squares on the screen with his finger, before he takes his turn*).
Sean:	1. It's there.
Lester:	So it has got to be…
Sean:	5, 4 (*suggesting co-ordinates*).
Lester:	(*ignoring Sean*).
	4, 3. No, we have had 4, 3.
Sean:	4, 5. No, 4, 4.
Lester:	4, 3 (*presses keys for his turn*) What! (*he fails to find the elephant*) That's easy, I know where it is, opposite.
	(*both sit silently for a while, looking at the screen*)
Lester:	I can do it.
Sean:	(*still staring at the screen*) No, not up, down.
Lester:	It can't be.
Sean:	It can.
Lester:	I know where it is.
	(*Sean eventually takes his turn, but fails to find the elephant*)
Lester:	I told you it weren't over there. (*He then takes his turn, without success*)
Sean:	Eh, heh heh heh (*laughing gleefully*).
Lester:	Which one just went on? I don't know (*says something unintelligible*).
Sean:	1, 2, 3, 4, 5, 6 (*counting squares*).
Lester:	I know where it is.
Sean:	I got the nearest.
Lester:	(*counting squares*) 1, 2, 3, 4, 5, 6, 7, 8.
Sean:	I got the nearest, 5.
Lester:	So it has got to be 1, 8.
Lester:	2, 8.
Sean:	Oh, suit yourself.

The second sequence is from a session in which two 10-year-old girls, Katie and Anne, were working on the production of their own class newspaper, using some desktop publishing software for schools called Front Page Extra.[30] They were friends, who had successfully worked together before. Their teacher had helped them load the program and set up the screen for their immediate task, which was to design and write their front page. At the point the sequence begins, they have been engaged in the task for about an hour and a quarter and are trying to compose some text for the front page.

Sequence 6.2: Fantabuloso

Katie:	Okay, so right then. What shall we write?
Anne:	We can have something like those autograph columns and things like that and items, messages.
Katie:	Inside these covers. (*pause*) Our fun-filled...
Anne:	That's it!
Katie:	Something...
Anne:	Something like that!
Katie:	Yeah.
Anne:	Inside this fabulous fun-filled covers are — how can we have a fun-filled cover? Let me try.
Katie:	Inside these (*long pause*)...
Anne:	Hah huh (*laughs*).
Anne:	You sound happy on this. Fantabuloso (*laughs*).
Katie:	Inside these, inside these fant, inside these fun-filled, no inside these covers these fantastic these brilliant...
Anne:	Brilliant...
Katie:	Is it brilliant?
Anne:	No.
Katie:	No. Fantast fantabuloso, shall we put that?
Anne:	Yeah (*says something inaudible*) fantabluloso.
Katie:	Fan-tab-u-lo-so.
Anne:	Loso. Fantabuloso.
Katie:	Fantabuloso oso.
Anne:	Fantabuloso ho!

The third sequence shows a group of three children aged 9–10 (two boys and a girl) using a program called Viking England, a kind of historical simulation package which allows children to take on the active roles of Viking raiders planning an invasion of the English coast. [31] They had all recently been working in different groups, but two of them had worked together before. In response to events and to questions which appeared on the screen, members of the 'raiding party' had to decide what resources were required for the raid, how to overcome the opposition through strategy, and so on. In this sequence they are trying to decide which of four possible sites they should raid (a monastery, a village of huts, a castle or a harbour).

Sequence 6.3: Planning a raid

Diana:	Let's discuss it. Which one shall we go for?
All:	(*inaudible — reading from instructions*)
Peter:	1, 2, 3 or 4 (*reading out the number of options available*). Well we've got no other chance of getting more money because…
Adrian:	And there's a monastery.
Diana:	And if we take number 2 there's that (*inaudible*)…
Peter:	Yeh but because the huts will be guarded.
All:	Yeh.
Adrian:	And that will probably be guarded.
Diana:	It's surrounded by trees.
Peter:	Yeh.
Adrian:	And there's a rock guarding us there.
Peter:	Yes there's some rocks there. So I think, I think it should be 1.
Adrian:	Because the monastery might be unguarded.
Diana:	Yes 1.
Adrian:	1 yeh.
Peter:	Yeh but what about 2? That, it might be not guarded. Just because there's huts there it doesn't mean it's not guarded, does it? What do you think?
Diana:	Yes, it doesn't mean it's not. It doesn't mean to say its **not** guarded does it. It may well be guarded. I think we should go for number 1 because I'm pretty sure it's not guarded.
Adrian:	Yeh.
Peter:	Ok, yes, number 1 (*he keys in 1 on keyboard*). No (*computer responds inappropriately*).
Adrian:	You have to use them numbers (*he points to the number keys on right of board, and Peter uses them to obtain the right result. Adrian begins to read from screen display*). 'You have chosen to raid area 1.'

I will now comment on each of the three sequences.

Comments on Sequence 6.1

In this sequence, we see two boys actively and enthusiastically engaged in their task. They argue about who knows best, sometimes trying to justify their claims by recourse to the evidence on the screen. They offer suggestions, comments and advice on each other's actions, and ask each other a few questions. In the session as a whole, there was a lot of talk, and it was all 'on task'. But consider the sequence as a piece of joint constructive problem-solving, and especially as one which would help the boys develop their ability to deal with problems in an 'educated' way, and its quality is doubtful. The talk nearly all consists of short assertions, rebuttals or comments which are not constructive. They ignore each other's remarks, and when one asks for information the other does not provide it. Superior knowledge is often claimed, but not offered helpfully. Sequence 6.1 was typical of most of the talk in this session. The amount of real collaboration — in the sense of sharing of ideas, joint evaluation of information, hypothesising and decision-making, or even taking any advice offered — was minimal. The boys effectively redefined this supposedly collaborative activity as a *competitive* one. They took alternate turns: but then so do opponents in tennis. In the session as a whole, each time they did the puzzle, whoever happened to key in the last pair of co-ordinates before the elephant was found, claimed this vociferously as a personal victory. It was difficult to see what either boy was learning about 'learning through talk', or about maths, from doing this activity. They both seemed to understand the concept of co-ordinates already, and their strategies did not seem to change or develop as they played.

Comments on Sequence 6.2

In this sequence, we see Katie and Anne talking through their text. They ask each other questions (though Anne's question 'how can we have a fun-filled cover?' seems more the expression of a problem rather than a request for information from her partner), they make suggestions and offer some reasons for the decisions they take. They confirm and validate each other's statements, explicitly ('That's it!') or implicitly by repeating them ('Inside these…'.). They are not only constructing their text together, they are constructing a joint understanding of what the text should be like. They clearly enjoy working together, perhaps reflecting a shared history of successful collaboration. There is only one real disagreement: they do not challenge each other's suggestions, and do not seem to feel the need to justify opinions or explain their reasons.

Comments on Sequence 6.3

In Sequence 6.3 we again see some children on task, asking each other questions, commenting and making suggestions. They discuss the various options, and also remind each other of relevant information. They are using talk to share information and plan together. They discuss and evaluate possible courses of action and make joint decisions. There is a lot of explicit reasoning in the talk. What is more, this reasoning is essentially *interactive* — not really reducible to the form and content of individual statements, but more to do with how the discourse as a whole represents a social, shared thought process. There was a lot of this kind of talk in the Viking England activity, in which the children seemed to be reasoning together and building up shared knowledge and understanding to a new level through their talk.

Three Ways of Talking and Thinking

I will now use the analysis of sequences 6.1–6.3 to typify three ways of talking and thinking.

1. The first way of talking is **Disputational talk**, which is characterised by disagreement and individualised decision-making. There are few attempts to pool resources, or to offer constructive criticism of suggestions. This is how Sean and Lester talk in Sequence 6.1. Disputational talk also has some characteristic discourse features — short exchanges consisting of assertions and challenges or counter-assertions.
2. Next there is **Cumulative talk**, in which speakers build positively but uncritically on what the other has said. Partners use talk to construct a 'common knowledge' by accumulation. Cumulative discourse is characterised by repetitions, confirmations and elaborations. We can see Katie and Anne talking like this in Sequence 6.2.
3. Last is **Exploratory talk**, in which partners engage critically but constructively with each other's ideas. Diana, Peter and Adrian talk like this in Sequence 6.3. Statements and suggestions are offered for joint consideration. These may be challenged and counter-challenged, but challenges are justified and alternative hypotheses are offered. Compared with the other two types, in exploratory talk *knowledge is made more publicly accountable* and *reasoning is more visible in the talk*. Progress then emerges from the eventual joint agreement reached.

'Disputational', 'cumulative' and 'exploratory' are not meant to be descriptive categories into which all observed speech can be neatly and separately coded. They are analytic categories, typifications of ways in which children in the SLANT project talked together. What I am attempting to do here is elaborate the concepts of disputational talk, cumulative talk and exploratory talk into models of three *distinctive social modes of thinking*, models which help us understand how actual talk (which is inevitably resistant to neat categorisation) is used by people to 'think together'.

Three levels of analysis

To describe and evaluate the actual talk which goes on in any collaborative educational activity, we need to incorporate the models of talk into an analysis which operates at three levels (I am using 'level' here to mean something like 'depth of focus'). The first level is *linguistic*: we examine the talk as spoken text. What kinds of 'speech acts' do the students perform? (Do they assert, challenge, explain, request?) What kinds of exchanges take place? (That is, how do speakers build their conversations, how do they respond and react to each other's talk?) What topics are discussed? It is at this level that we can see that 'disputational talk' typifies talk dominated by assertions and counter-assertions, with few of the repetitions and elaborations which characterise 'cumulative talk'. 'Exploratory talk', in comparison, typifies talk which combines challenges and requests for clarification with responses which provide explanations and justifications.[32]

The second level is *psychological*: an analysis of the talk as thought and action. What kinds of 'ground rules' do the speakers seem to be following? How do the ways the speakers interact, the topics they discuss and the issues they raise, reflect their interests and concerns?[33] To what extent is reasoning visibly being pursued through the talk? We may be able to use the models of talk to typify the kind of communicative relationship that the speakers are acting out, and the ground rules that they use to do so. So, for example, in disputational talk the relationship is competitive; information is flaunted rather than shared, differences of opinion are stressed rather than resolved, and the general orientation is defensive. Cumulative talk seems to operate more on implicit concerns with solidarity and trust, and the ground rules seem to require the constant repetition and confirmation of partners' ideas and opinions. Exploratory talk foregrounds reasoning. Its ground rules require that the views of all participants are sought and considered, that proposals are explicitly stated and evaluated, and that explicit agreement precedes decisions and actions. Both cumulative and exploratory talk seem to be aimed at the achievement of consensus while disputational talk does not. In disputational talk, although a lot of interaction may be going on, the reasoning involved is very individualised and tacit. In cumulative talk, by comparison, ideas and information are certainly shared and joint decisions may be reached; but there is little in the way of challenge or constructive conflict in the process of constructing knowledge. Exploratory talk, by incorporating both conflict and the open sharing of ideas represents the more 'visible' pursuit of rational consensus through conversation. More than the other two types, it is like the kind of talk which has been found to be most effective for solving problems through collaborative activity (as discussed on page 98).

If we want to make some judgements about the educational value of any observed talk, an additional level of analysis is needed. This could be called the *cultural* level, because it inevitably involves some consideration of the nature of 'educated' discourse and of the kinds of reasoning that are valued and encouraged in the cultural institutions of formal education. And here, it seems to me, the analytic category of exploratory talk deserves special attention. It typifies language which embodies certain principles — of accountability, of clarity, of constructive criticism and receptiveness to well-argued proposals — which are valued highly in many societies. In many of our key social institutions — for example, the law, government administration, research in the sciences and arts, and the negotiation of business — people have to use language to interrogate the quality of the claims, hypotheses and proposals made by other people, to express clearly their own understandings, to reach consensual agreement and make joint decisions.[34]

Some psychologists and language researchers have suggested that educated discourse is unlike much everyday discourse because it is 'disembedded' or 'decontextualised', so that words are dealt with free of context, in terms of abstract meanings. For example, Margaret Donaldson suggests that the essence of the most advanced kinds of intellectual thought and language is 'the ability to attend to the meanings of words themselves'.[35] However, 'decontextualisation' seems an unsuitable term for describing the essence of educated discourse. Look, for example, at one kind of educated discourse, the language of a country's legal system. Donaldson gives this as an example of a detached, decontextualised mode of language use. But legal language stands upon a vast foundation of history, and making sense of it as a professional takes years of training in the conventions of courts and legal documents and a knowledge of events (e.g. important court cases) which have gone before. The language of the professionals in any court room, or in any legal document, is a heavily contextualised form of discourse. Lawyers are expected to make their statements accountable to canons of law and to justify assertions by presenting evidence. The language that Donaldson and others call 'decontextualised' or 'disembedded' has, I would say, two quite different characteristics: it is language in which *reasoning is made visible* and in which *knowledge is made accountable* — not in any absolute terms, but in accord with the 'ground rules' of the relevant discourse community.

I would, however, like to retain one central and important element of the arguments made by Donaldson and others. This is that if we encourage and enable children to use language in certain ways — to ask certain kinds of questions, to clearly describe events, to account for outcomes and consolidate what they have learned in words — we are helping them understand and gain access to educated discourse. Of course, there is much more involved in taking active part in any 'educated discourse' than using talk in an 'exploratory' way. There is the accumulated knowledge, the specialised vocabulary and other conventions of any particular discourse community to take account of. But exploratory talk represents qualities that are a vital, basic part of many educated discourses. Encouraging it may help learners develop intellectual habits that will serve them well across a range of different situations.

It might seem that I am suggesting that children — students — should have yet another alien set of 'ground rules' imposed on them, but that is not so. The following sequence comes from a discussion between Eunice Fisher (one of the SLANT researchers) and a group of four six-year-olds in one of the project schools. She was trying to discover their views on the value of 'discussion'. The children have already said that they sometimes discuss things when they work together.

Sequence 6.4: What do you do with discussion?

Researcher: And then what would you hope to do by discussing it, what do you think that you would get in the end?

Peter: It would help you by telling you what — making people agree with you, so we've got, um, well — making people agree with you, letting people agree, um, so we got, so we've got two people who want the same thing.
(*and later, talking about activity outside the classroom*)

Researcher: Angela, what about you? Do you discuss things outside too?

Angela: Well, when we don't think something's, um, when I don't think, when we don't think something's right in the game, we just actually have to stop it and discuss what is, what is happening, what's the wrong thing.

Researcher: Suppose you disagree, what happens then?

Angela: Pardon (*other children are talking*)?

Researcher: Supposing, supposing you say something and your friend that you're discussing it with says the opposite, what do you do next, what do you do then?

Angela: You have to discuss something which is like, half what the other person says and half (*gestures two 'portions' with her hands*) which is what you said.

Researcher: Right.

Angela: Yes, you just put it together so that it's... (*as her speech tails off, she brings her hands together*).

In this extract, some very young schoolchildren try to explain an important function of language which is difficult to put into words. You can see the thinking process in the unfinished phrases, the false starts and the 'ums'. But they are talking about real experience, and that experience is the basis of exploratory talk. There is no evidence from research to show that anyone is incapable of exploratory talk. What is more, there is no reason to assume that the basic principles of exploratory talk are alien to children. The ideal of a speech situation in which everyone is free to express their views, and in which the most reasonable views gain general acceptance, is implicit in many areas of social life. Even if people often violate the principles involved, they are still invoked as ideals.

Encouraging Exploratory Talk

I now want to consider the role of a teacher in encouraging the use of certain ways of talking. By the time that the SLANT project had been running for about a year, it had become clear that for many of the recorded sessions both teachers and researchers (who had reviewed the recordings) were disappointed with the quality of talk which had taken place. The kind of talk which we came to typify as 'exploratory' occurred sporadically and only occasionally throughout the sessions. In most sessions, the children rarely seemed to spend much time considering and evaluating information, ideas were often only partially expressed and, in some pairs and groups, partners seemed to ignore each other's views, or the talk and decision-making was dominated by a few of the group members. Also, the children involved seemed to be operating disparate sets of ground rules for doing collaborative activities at the computer. For example, while some seemed to feel that the views of all partners should influence decisions, others seemed to assume that decision-making lay with the person operating the keyboard. Yet others seemed to define the keyboard operator as merely a clerk, with most contributions of ideas and instructions coming from others in the group acting in an 'executive' capacity. Some partners insisted on passing the keyboard between them after each 'go', while others used longer-term divisions of labour. These matters were discussed at length by teachers and researchers, and in accord with the 'action research' philosophy which informed the project, this led to some of the teachers designing new, different kinds of activities.

In the school in which sequences 6.1–6.3 were recorded, this discussion resulted in the following plan for action. First, researchers and the teacher selected one educational computer program (from those in use in the school) which seemed to provide a good basis for a collaborative activity which would *require* the children to share information and make joint decisions. This was Viking England, as described at the beginning of Sequence 6.3. Teacher and researchers then discussed what ground rules the children might be encouraged to follow, though the final decision about what these would be and how they would be presented was left with the teacher. She eventually decided that she would stress the importance of:

- sharing all relevant information and suggestions;
- having to provide reasons to back up assertions and opinions and suggestions;
- asking for reasons when appropriate;
- reaching agreement about what action to take, if at all possible;
- accepting that the group (rather than any individual member) was responsible for decisions and actions and for any successes and failures which ensued.[36]

The teacher then planned for her class some awareness-raising activities on talk and collaborative activity, away from the computer. Eight three-person groups were set up by the teacher. Each group included at least one child with special needs in literacy, another who was an able and fluent reader, and consideration was taken of how children's personal styles and relationships in the class might affect who would work best together. In their groups, the children then did some activities intended to raise their awareness of the nature and quality of classroom discussion. These were taken and adapted from some published material on 'oracy' for teachers,[37] and included such activities as:

(a) Listening to a tape of sound effects. The group had to try to decide together what they thought each was, nominate a 'writer' to record their ideas and then report back to the class.

(b) Each child had to describe to their group an event that had happened to them during their Christmas holiday. One of the listeners then re-told the story to the class.

(c) Two of the group sat back-to-back and one of them had a minute to draw a shape or pattern. That person then described the shape and the other had to draw it from this description (with other group members as an attentive audience).

The teacher also led some group and class discussions about 'arguments', 'taking turns' and other topics related to taking part in conversations. Through picking up ideas and opinions offered by the children, the teacher was able to gain some insights into the children's current understanding of how discussions should be conducted. She was also able to make clear some of her own ideas on how groups should operate, to which the children seemed quite receptive. She continued to stress the need for all relevant views to be heard, for agreement to be sought if possible, and for groups rather than individuals to feel responsible for decisions reached and actions pursued.

The children then went on to do collaborative activities at the computer, in pairs or groups of three. But before each group began this activity, the teacher reminded them of the earlier activities and encouraged each of these new sets of children to explicitly rehearse the 'ground rules' for discussion that they would follow. The result was a dramatic increase in the amount of 'exploratory' talk in these groups, in comparison with earlier recorded activities. It also seemed that the enthusiasm and involvement of the children were improved. It is worth stressing that this particular school is not one with a 'privileged' catchment area: the housing estate surrounding it has more than its share of social problems and the effects of unemployment, and the children involved in the project included some with recognised social and psychological problems. One of the children in Sequence 6.3 was in fact facing possible exclusion from the school for persistent bad behaviour.

I have concentrated here on the apparent effects of the teacher's preparatory work (the talk awareness activities and the ways she set up the groups) rather than the contribution made by the Viking England computer software. The choice of that software, or at least that kind of software, was probably very important for the success of the initial activity.[38] But the ground rules that were established in this way were not just used for Viking England, and were successfully applied by the children in other, non-computer-based activities. The next sequence was recorded some months later, when the same teacher was rehearsing the ground rules with a group of 10-year-olds who were about to begin an activity (not computer-based) in which they had to identify various animals of the Brazilian rain forest. She has just established that they have all the pictures of animals that they require (I have marked words she stresses in bold type).

Sequence 6.5: Rehearsing the ground rules

Teacher: The next thing you've got to do is to decide **between** you which is which. So if you have a reason for thinking that's *(holding up a picture of a manatee)* a scarlet macaw you say 'I think it is because it has flippers'*(children laugh)*. So you then you would have to accept someone else's opinion if it was different from yours, so you would say something like ' Do you agree?' *(one boy says 'no')* or 'I think that's wrong' *(boy*

says 'yes'). And the person who was going to disagree with
you wouldn't just say 'no', you would have to have a reason
for disagreeing. What (*addressing Paul, the boy who spoke last*)
would be your reason for disagreeing with that (*she shows him
the picture*) being a scarlet macaw?

Paul: Because macaws don't have flippers.
Oliver: Because the macaw is a parrot! (*laughing*)
Teacher: Right. Whatever point of view you want to put over, you will
have to try to think of your reason for giving it.

The children then went on to do the activity, and the next sequence is an
extract from a late stage when they were trying to classify all the animals
as either 'herbivores' or 'carnivores'.

Sequence 6.6: Classifying animals

Emmeline: Now we've got a fish — uh — the...
Oliver: What sort, the piranha?
Emmeline: No, the little, not the scaly one.
Maddy: Lun, lungf...(*hesitating*)
Oliver: Lungfish.
Maddy: It probably feeds on things in the river, because it's not going
to go out and catch a monkey or something, is it? (*all laugh*)
Emmeline: Yeah. Could bri...
Oliver: (*interrupting*) There is of course river plants, some of them do
feed on river plants, and leaves that fall in the river.
Maddy: Yeah, it's probably a herbivore.
Ben: We haven't got anything to tell.
Emmeline: What do you think it should be?
Oliver: No, actually I think we should put it in 'carnivore', most fish
are.
Emmeline: No, because, ma...
Oliver: (*interrupting*) It's our best, and most fish are, isn't it?
Emmeline: (*interrupting*) Yeah, but we've got this one here, and this one
here (*she indicates some fish cards in both 'carnivore' and
'herbivore' piles on the table*).
[*The discussion continues, unresolved, until Ben says...*]
Ben: Let's have a vote, have a vote.
Emmeline: Yeah, let's have a vote.
Ben: (*to Oliver*) What do you think?
Oliver: I think 'carnivore'.
Ben: (*to Maddy*) What do you reckon?

Maddy: I think 'herbivore'.
Ben: (*to Emmeline*) What do you reckon?
Emmeline: 'Herbivore'.
Oliver: What do you reckon? (*to Ben*)
Ben: (*laughing, looking sheepish and uncertain, doesn't answer*)
Oliver: Come on, this isn't worth it, it's a lungf...
Ben: Carnivore.
Oliver: Carnivore, that's two each.
Ben: Let's, OK (*he prepares to toss a coin*).
Oliver: No, don't bother flipping a coin, it's meant to be.
Ben: (*interrupts, tosses coin*) Flip.
Oliver: ...thinking!
Ben: Heads or tails?
Oliver: Lung, no, shush!
Emmeline: It's heads. Well, you win.
Oliver: (*picks up the 'lungfish' card and reads*) 'The lungfish has a pair
                 or lungs and small gills and burrows in the mud and breathes
                 air.' It can't be a herbivore because what would it eat when
                 it's on its own in the sand? There's nothing to eat.

The children then resumed their debate about the lungfish, and eventually decided that they had insufficient information and would leave the card separate and return to it 'at the end' when the teacher returned. The session which provided Sequence 6.6 was not a perfect model of equitable, rational discussion: in their excitement the children sometimes interrupted each other, the boys sometimes tried to dominate proceedings, and the reasons given for making decisions were not always valid. But there was certainly a lot of exploratory talk, as illustrated in the sequence. We can see that the children ask each other questions, they appeal for everyone's views, they try to justify their views rationally and by recourse to evidence. They try to reach agreement through the democratic process of a vote. When that fails, Ben does propose (with Emmeline's support) that they resolve the dilemma through the non-rational process of tossing a coin. But notice then what Oliver does — he objects, reminds the group of the ground rules agreed for the activity ('it's meant to be *thinking!*') and pulls in some additional relevant information for the group's consideration. Faced with this appeal, the children resume their rational debate.

I have given just one example, from one school, of how talk of an 'exploratory' type was encouraged amongst learners. My purpose is simply to illustrate a possibility made real, achieved through the sharing of knowledge between researchers, teachers and learners. But evidence for the importance of helping learners acquire, understand, use and appreciate the value of ground rules for conducting discussions which are rational, equitable and productive is emerging from sociocultural research elsewhere. Baker-Sennett, Matusov and Rogoff give the following example of an American teacher rehearsing some similar ground rules for a group of girls aged 7–9 who are going to perform their own version of the story of Snow White:

Teacher:	You'll vote as a group and you'll say, 'OK, do we want to do it the old way or the modern way?' and everyone will have to discuss it and say the pros and the cons. When having a little group there are certain things that make it hard. One guy has an idea and says, 'MODERN, MODERN! I want it modern'. Does that help the group?
Kids:	(*in unison*): No!
Teacher:	Or if some kids just sit there and don't say anything, does that help the group?
Kids:	(*in unison*): No!
Teacher:	OK, so you have to figure out a way to make the group work. What if I said, 'I have seen groups that have too many chiefs and no indians?' What do I mean? Leslie...
Leslie:	That means that too many people are taking over the group.
Teacher:	Everybody want to be the boss and nobody listens. So that might be a problem that you might have to solve with your group. Because you might always need some workers and some listeners. Part of this will be figuring out how to make your group work...There will be some adults in the room to help but a lot of the time it will just be up to you to say 'wait a minute, we need to compromise' or 'we need to vote on it', rather than just one guy taking over.[39]

Notice that, in both this example and in Sequence 6.5: *Rehearsing the ground rules*, the teachers use some of the well-established techniques for guidance that I described in Chapter 3 (see especially Table 1). Both sequences are attempts by teachers to draw out from the children some salient information from their past shared experience. Both teachers try to *elicit* aspects of the ground rules from the children, and in so doing are asking 'closed' questions to which they know the answers. The first teacher explicitly *confirms* the correctness of Paul and Oliver's responses with the comment 'Right'. The second teacher *reformulates* Leslie's response, so as to make her (the teacher's) intended point more clearly. Some people might see both sequences as unfortunate examples of teachers doing most of the talking, constraining children's responses and imposing the teacher's own interpretation of ground rules on children's activities. I see them as examples of teachers doing the job they are expected to do, of guiding the construction of knowledge.

Summary and Conclusions

Although talk amongst learners has tended to have low status in formal education, recent research provides some good reasons for encouraging learners to talk and work together in educational activities. However, research does not support the idea that talk and collaboration are inevitably useful, or that learners left to their own devices necessarily know how to make best use of their opportunities. A sociocultural perspective on classroom education supports the use of collaborative activity, but it also highlights the need for a rationale, in terms of both procedures and principles, for the activities learners are expected to do as part of their education. What is more, learners themselves need access to that rationale; and it has to be a rationale that they find convincing. Of course, learners, even those young ones entering infant school, are never 'blank slates' on which their teachers must inscribe all educationally relevant skills. Children over 9 or 10 may have learned all the language strategies they need to engage in exploratory talk (and so in educated discourse) without having been taught them. They may well already use them to good effect on occasion (research like Janet Maybin's suggests that children have more opportunity for explaining and justifying in their informal conversations than they normally do when they are 'on task' in class).[40] But they need guidance on how to use talk. There are good reasons to believe that pupils and students are often unsure or unaware of what they are expected to be doing and achieving in educational activities, and that teachers often provide little useful information about such things to them. It cannot be assumed that learners already possess a good understanding and awareness of how best to go about 'learning together' in the classroom.

I know that I have not given much space here to such matters as children's social identities and personal histories, which are important for the organisation and evaluation of any collaborative activity. But there are communicative and intellectual dimensions to the organisation of collaborative activities which are also important if the activities are intended to contribute to children's educational progress. Simply sitting them down with a shared task may stimulate talk, but of what kind and quality? It may be that too often the organiser of collaborative activities does not have a clear notion of what kind of talk they are trying to encourage and for what reason. As Terry Phillips [41] points out, 'Why?' is a neglected question in planning collaborative activity. Teachers may take the ground rules for granted or, perhaps under the influence of a 'progressive' educational ideology, they may think that is wrong to guide students' activity so precisely. Too often learners have to try to make sense of the activity as best they can, being given little help in understanding and appreciating the ground rules they are expected to follow. How can we expect them then to make the rules their own?

I have suggested that it is possible to identify particular ways of talking that represent different social modes of thinking, and I have argued that it is both desirable and possible to encourage learners to use some of those ways of talking to construct knowledge together. It is also necessary for teachers and learners to establish some agreement about what 'talk' in the classroom is for and how it should be conducted. There is evidence from other research as well as my own to support this view. But there is no evidence to suggest that such preparation for collaborative activity is a normal part of life in most schools or other educational institutions, anywhere in the world.

Notes

1 On the subject of 'keeping 'em quiet', see Denscombe, M. (1985) *Classroom Control: A Sociological Perspective*. London: Allen & Unwin.

2 For a discussion of this aspect of Piaget's work and its relationship to other research on collaborative learning, see Light, P. and Littleton, K. (1994) Cognitive approaches to group work. In P. Kutnick and C. Rogers (eds) *Groups in Schools*. London: Cassell.

3 See for example Bell, N., Grossen, M. and Perret-Clermont, A-N. (1985) Socio-cognitive conflict and intellectual growth. In M.W. Berkowitz (ed.) *Peer Conflict and Psychological Growth (New Directions in Child Development no.29)*. San Francisco: Jossey-Bass. Also Doise, W. and Mugny, G. (1984) *The Social Development of Intellect*. Oxford: Pergamon Press.

4 See, for example, Wells, G. (1992) The centrality of talk in education. In K. Norman (ed.) *Thinking Voices: The Work of the National Oracy Project*. London: Hodder & Stoughton.

5 Bruner, J. (1985) Vygotsky: A historical and conceptual perspective. In J. Wertsch (ed.) *Culture, Communication and Cognition: Vygotskian Perspectives* (p. 24). Cambridge: Cambridge University Press.

6 See for example Fletcher, B. (1985) Group and individual learning of junior school children on a microcomputer-based task. *Educational Review* 37, 251–61; and Hoyles, C., Sutherland, R. and Healy, I. (1990) Children talking in computer environments: New insights on the role of discussion in mathematics learning. In K. Durkin and B. Shine (eds) *Language and Mathematics Education*. Milton Keynes: Open University Press.

7 Galton, M., Simon, B. and Croll, P. (1980) *Inside the Primary Classroom (the ORACLE Project)*. London: Routledge & Kegan Paul.

8 Galton, M. and Williamson, J. (1992) *Group work in the Primary Classroom* (p.43). London: Routledge.

9   See Open University (1991) *Talk and Learning 5–16: An In-service Pack on Oracy for Teachers*. Milton Keynes: The Open University, which contains many case studies and also an audiocassette of children engaged in a wide range of talk activities; also K. Norman (ed.) *Thinking Voices: The Work of the National Oracy Project*. London: Hodder & Stoughton.

10 See for example Light and Glachan's studies of children doing the 'Tower of Hanoi' problem. Light, P. and Glachan, M. (1985) Facilitation of problem-solving through peer interaction. *Educational Psychology* 5, 217–25.

11 See Barbieri, M. and Light, P. (1992) Interaction, gender and performance on a computer-based task. *Learning and Instruction* 2, 199–213. Also Light (1991) Peers, problem-solving and computers. *Golem* 3 (1), 2–6; Blaye, A., Light, P., Joiner R. and Sheldon, S. (1991) Collaboration as facilitator of planning and problem-solving on a computer-based task. *British Journal of Developmental Psychology* 9, 471–83; Light, P. (1993) Collaborative learning with computers. In P. Scrimshaw (ed.) *Language, Classrooms and Computers*. London: Routledge; and Light and Littleton (1994, see note 2 above).

12 Light, P., Littleton, K., Messer, D. and Joiner, R. (1994) Social and communicative processes in computer-based problem-solving. *European Journal of Psychology of Education* 9 (2), 93–110; and Messer, D., Joiner, R., Light, P. and Littleton, K. (1993) Influences on the effectiveness of peer interaction: Children's level of cognitive development and the relative ability of partners. *Social Development* 2 (3), 279–94. See also Hoyles, C, Healy, L. and Pozzi, S. (1992). Interdependence and autonomy: Aspects of groupwork with computers. *Learning and Instruction* 2, 239–57.

13 See for example Lave, J. (1992) Word problems: A microcosm of theories of learning. In P. Light and G. Butterworth (eds) *Context and Cognition: Ways of Learning and Knowing*. Hemel Hempstead: Harvester-Wheatsheaf.

14 For a discussion of 'procedural/principled' understanding, see Chapter 6 of Edwards, D. and Mercer, N. (1987) *Common Knowledge*. London: Methuen/Routledge.

15 Hatano, G. and Inagaki, K. (1992) Desituating cognition through the construction of conceptual knowledge. In P. Light and G. Butterworth (eds) *Context and Cognition: Ways of Learning and Knowing*. Hemel Hempstead: Harvester-Wheatsheaf.

16 Barnes, D. and Todd, F. (1977) *Communication and Learning in Small Groups*. London: Routledge & Kegan Paul. (A new edition of this book is expected in 1995.)

17 Barnes and Todd (1977, note 16) p. 127.

18 Barnes and Todd (1977, note 16) p. 67.

19 Barnes and Todd (1977, note 16) p. 75

20 Barnes and Todd (1977, note 16) p. 73.

21 See Galton and Williamson's (1992, note 8) review of research.

22 See Light and Littleton (1994, note 2); also Pozzi, S., Healy, L. and Hoyles, C. (1993) Learning and interaction in groups with computers: When do ability and gender matter? *Social Development* 3 (3), pp. 233–41.

23 Swann, J. (1992) *Girls, Boys and Language*. London: Blackwell.

24 Swann, J. (1994) What do we do about gender? In B. Stierer and J. Maybin (eds) *Language, Literacy and Learning in Educational Practice*. Clevedon: Multilingual Matters.

25 See Swann, J. (1992) as in note 23.

26 See Pozzi, S., Healy, L. and Hoyles, C. (1993) Learning and interaction in groups with computers: When do ability and gender matter? *Social Development* 2 (3), 222–41.

27 Azmitia, M. and Montgomery, R. (1993) Friendship, transactive dialogues, and the development of scientific reasoning. *Social Development* 2 (3), 202–21.

28 SLANT was a joint venture of the University of East Anglia and the Open University, funded by the Economic and Social Research Council. It involved schools in Buckinghamshire, Cambridgeshire, Northamptonshire and Norfolk. For a brief account of the project, see Mercer, N. (1994b) The quality of talk in children's joint activity at the computer. *Journal of Computer Assisted Learning* 10, 24–32. See also note 33 below. For a more general socio-cultural perspective on computers and learning, see Scrimshaw, P. (1993) (ed.) *Language, Classrooms and Computers*. London: Routledge.

29 The 'Smile' software was produced by the Inner London Education Authority in 1984.

30 'Front Page Extra' was produced by R. Keeling, Newman College, in 1988 and distributed by Buckinghamshire County Council.

31 'Viking England' was produced by Fernleaf Educational Software Ltd., Gravesend.

32 Terry Phillips uses the term 'exploratory talk' to describe only the preliminary stages of examining and sharing information, and uses 'argumentative talk' for the process of debate itself (Phillips, T., 1990, Structuring talk for exploratory talk. In D. Wray (ed.) *Talking and Listening*. London: Scholastic. However, I feel that the term 'argumentative' has negative, disputational connotations. I believe that I am using the term 'exploratory' in a similar way to Douglas Barnes, in Barnes, D. (1992) The role of talk in learning. In K. Norman (ed.) *Thinking Voices*. London: Hodder & Stoughton.

33 See Edwards, D. (in press) Towards a discursive psychology of classroom education. In C. Coll (ed.) *Classroom Discourse*. Madrid: Infancia y Aprendizaje.

34 This scheme of analysis emerged from work with Rupert Wegerif, but also draws heavily on the work of Eunice Fisher, Terry Phillips, Peter Scrimshaw and all involved in the SLANT project (though they are not responsible for any inadequacies). See in particular Fisher, E. (1993) Distinctive features of pupil–pupil classroom talk and their relationship to learning. *Language and Education* 7 (4), 239–58; and Wegerif, R. (1994) Educational software and the quality of children's talk, *Centre for Language and Communications Occasional Papers No. 40*. Milton Keynes: The Open University.

35 Donaldson, M. (1992) *Human Minds*. London: Allen Lane. See also Donaldson, M. (1978) *Children's Minds*. London: Fontana; and Wells, G. (1986) *The Meaning Makers* (Chapter 8). London: Hodder & Stoughton.

36 For fuller accounts of this activity by the teacher and researchers involved, see Dawes, L., Mercer, N. and Fisher, E. (1992) The quality of talk at the computer. *Language and Learning*, October 1992; and Dawes, L. (1993) Special report: Talking points. *Junior Education*, February 1993.

37 Brooks, G., Latham, J. and Rex, A. (1986) *Developing Oral Skills*. London: Heinemann. Also Open University (1991) *Talk and Learning 5–16: An In-Service Pack on Oracy for Teachers*. Milton Keynes: The Open University.

38 For a discussion of possible effects of software on talk, see publications listed in note 28 above.

39 Baker-Sennett, J., Matusov, E. and Rogoff, B. (1992) Sociocultural processes of creative planning in children's playcrafting. In P. Light and G. Butterworth (eds) *Context and Cognition: Ways of Learning and Knowing*. Hemel Hempstead: Harvester-Wheatsheaf. See also Lyle, S. (1993) An investigation into ways in which children 'talk themselves into meaning'. *Language and Education* 7 (3), 181–97; and Berrill, D. (1991) Exploring underlying assumptions: Small group work of university undergraduates. *Educational Review* 43 (2), 143–57.
40 Maybin, J. (1994) Children's voices: Talk, knowledge and identity. In D. Graddol, J. Maybin and B. Stierer (eds) *Researching Language and Literacy in Social Context*. Clevedon: Multilingual Matters.
41 Phillips, T. (1992) Why? The neglected question in planning for small group work. In K. Norman (ed.) *Thinking Voices*. London: Hodder & Stoughton. See also Sheeran, Y. and Barnes, D. (1991) *School Writing: Discovering the Ground Rules*. Milton Keynes: Open University Press. Also Westgate, D. and Corden, R. (1993) What we thought about things: Expectations, context and small group talk. *Language in Education* 7 (2), 115–26; Barnes, D. and Sheeran, Y. (1992) Oracy and genre. In K. Norman (ed.) *Thinking Voices*. London: Hodder & Stoughton.

7   Teachers, Researchers and the Construction of Knowledge

In recent years, discontent with the traditional relationship between those who do research on teaching and those who teach has encouraged the growth of what is known as 'educational action research'.[1] There are several versions of it, but what they have in common is the principle of asserting and privileging the perspective of the teacher, who then takes on the reflexive role of researcher of their own practice. Most action research is applied research, self-consciously aimed at improving practice. Work with the National Oracy Project and other educational and occupational training projects has given me close contact with this kind of research. As Sequence 2.4 (Chapter 2) showed, I have also done some research on my own practice as a teacher. I recognise the strengths of the action research approach. Through active involvement in research, teachers can 'see' their own classrooms and gain critical insights which they probably never would from reading the reports of more 'objective' researchers. This can lead teacher-researchers first to a sense of uncertainty in the hitherto taken-for-granted, and then on to a greater confidence and authority in their own practice. One important strand of the educational action research movement has also been the establishment of communication networks in which teacher-researchers can share their experiences, insights and practical propositions for change, because, like all practitioners, teachers listen and respond to the analyses and suggestions of fellow-teachers in ways that they never would to the advice of external 'experts'. However, I have two significant reservations about some of the educational action research I have encountered. The first is that it tends to celebrate awareness amongst practitioners, rather than encouraging engagement with critical ideas from outside their privileged perspective. And the second is that its advocates tend to set it up as oppositional to other more 'detached' kinds of research, and to define any entry by an external researcher into the process as almost inevitably coercive and disruptive, and antithetical to the emancipation of teachers as researchers.[2]

My own view is that the kind of applied action research which has most potential, in a whole range of fields as well as education, is socio-cultural research in which practitioners and external researchers work in *research partnership*, each contributing their expertise and experience. The gathering and analysis of data must take account of the different and potentially conflicting perspectives and agendas of each partner. For this to happen, there has to be some negotiation of what aims and agendas are being pursued, and of course the relationship has to be one of mutual trust. My colleagues and I developed a research partnership of this kind with teachers in the SLANT project (which was described briefly in the previous chapter). The essence of our approach was to try to merge the 'academic' research agenda of the team of 5 researchers with the curriculum-related professional goals of the 15 teachers involved. The researchers' interests in the use of talk in computer-based activities had generated the project, and so these inevitably focused and limited the scope of observations and analysis. But to say that the researchers set the agenda would not do justice to the way the project developed. Our interest in talk had been shaped by the work of teacher-researchers in the National Oracy Project,[3] and the activities we observed in the SLANT schools were planned and organised by the teachers in accord with their usual curriculum goals. Once the research was under way, regular meetings between teachers and researchers (which usually involved viewing of recently-recorded data) often led to new activities being designed, to the emergence of new themes in the analysis and to further cycles of activity, recording and analysis. Researchers and teachers also talked about the activities with the children involved. Our efforts were more successful than I had expected, if less so than I had dared to hope.[4] The partnership enabled dialogues about the analysis of data to continue throughout the project, with criteria for evaluating talk being explicitly and jointly considered, and some of the teachers used the results of analysis and evaluation to develop new kinds of classroom practice and shared these with other teachers outside the project. Those SLANT teachers have continued to be active in research since the project ended. As an applied researcher I am very aware of the value of the kind of dialogue that the research partnership provided, and will try to build the same kind of relationship into any future research. There were problems in sustaining dialogues between teachers and researchers, but these were more to do with research budgets and the impossible demands which work makes on the time of British primary teachers than with the incompatibility of researcher and teacher perspectives. In a different political world in which educational research was highly valued, and in which teachers' own enthusiasm for researching, evaluating and improving their own practice was recognised and justly rewarded, such difficulties would not be hard to overcome.

The dialogue between teachers and researchers can itself be analysed from a socio-cultural perspective; conversations between the partners in the research are opportunities for interests to be asserted, information to be shared, plans to be jointly formulated, interpretations to be disputed, and so on. The aim, once again, is the joint construction of new knowledge and understanding through talk. This knowledge is then applied to the design and evaluation of classroom activities and further research of the process of teaching and learning. The possibilities are there for involving learners, too, in the exploration of how teaching-and-learning is best carried out.

Language and the Construction of Knowledge

It may well be the case that a significant part of what we know, the information that we hold individually and collectively, is not constructed by our use of language.[5] It is obviously true that people can learn and develop their understanding, and do so with some success, without the benefit of talking with another person as they do so. The construction of knowledge is not a homogeneous process, and the conversations I have presented and analysed in this book illustrate just some of the ways that it happens. Even within the scope of my interest in how talk is used in classrooms and other similar settings, I know that there are important aspects of the construction of knowledge that my examples and analysis do not properly deal with. Those I am most aware of are the relationship between spoken language and written texts, the organisation of a classroom and its effects on talk, and the influence of personal identities and social relationships on even the most 'intellectual' conversations. Perhaps it will also seem to some people that I, like others of a neo-Vygotskian persuasion, emphasise continuity, co-operation and sharing in the construction of knowledge at the expense of individuality, conflict and creativity.[6] All these 'missing' topics and issues deserve their own place and time, and their own books. But their claims for attention do not undermine the importance of the central, basic themes of the book — how talk is used to guide the construction of knowledge, how teaching-and-learning happens in class-rooms, and how students gain access to intellectual communities of discourse which, for them, are new.

Socio-cultural research seems to me to offer the best means and opportunities for exploring these basic themes, and probably many others in the study of language and thought. One of the special attractions of the socio-cultural perspective is that it is reflexive — it accounts for the research process itself. It recognises that a researcher who observes and analyses talk is essentially just another language-user, a listener, a passive participant in the process of teaching and learning. The researcher's aim is to understand what the active participants understand, and to use the same means that they use — language — to do so. And in doing so, the researcher ceases to be a mere passive observer, not only because they become part of the context of the process that they are observing, but because to make their analysis they inevitably have to engage in talk with the people they are observing. This is how it is for all research on language and thinking, though many theories and research methods do not admit it explicitly. And to admit it does not mean the sad loss of 'objectivity' but rather the beginning of transforming research into a process in which traditional distinctions between 'practitioners' and 'researchers' no longer apply.

Notes

1   'Action research' is a method of applied research devised by Kurt Lewin. 'Educational action research' owes much to the efforts of Lawrence Stenhouse and others such as John Elliot, Steven Kemmis and Bridget Somekh in engaging teachers in research and the development of their own practice. See for example Elliot, J. (1991) *Action Research for Educational Change*. Milton Keynes: Open University Press; and the journal *Educational Action Research* edited at the University of East Anglia. For a critical review of this paradigm, see Hammersley, M. (1993) On the teacher as researcher. In M. Hammersley (ed.) *Educational Research: Current Issues*. London: Paul Chapman with the Open University.

2   For a strong statement of this point of view see Kemmis, S. (1993) Action research. In M. Hammersley (ed.) *Educational Research: Current Issues*. London: Paul Chapman with the Open University.

3   See for example Madeley, B. and Lautman, A. (1991) I like the way we learn; Steel, D. (1991) Granny's garden; and Prentice, M. (1991) A community of enquiry; all in *Talk and Learning 5–16: An In-Service Pack on Oracy for Teachers*. Milton Keynes: The Open University.

4   For joint accounts of SLANT research by teachers and researchers, see Dawes, L., Mercer, N. and Fisher, E. (1992) The quality of talk at the computer. *Language and Learning*, October 1992. For a teacher's account, see Dawes, L. (1993) Special Report: Talking points. *Junior Education*, February 1993.

5   Albert Einstein is a source of introspective evidence for claims that intellect is not necessarily language-based, as he said that his creative thought consisted of 'abstract images' rather than words. See A. Einstein (1968) Letter to Jacques Hadamard. In B. Ghiselin (ed.) *The Creative Process*. Mentor: New York.

6   For criticism of this kind see Engestrom, Y. (1991) Activity theory and individual and social transformation. *Activity Theory* 7–8, 6–17.

References

Arthur, J. (1992) Talking like teachers: Teacher and pupil discourse in Standard Six Botswana classrooms. *Centre for Language in Social Life, Working Paper No. 26.* University of Lancaster.

Azmitia, M. and Montgomery, R. (1993) Friendship, transactive dialogues, and the development of scientific reasoning. *Social Development* 2 (3), 202–21.

Baker-Sennett, J., Matusov, E. and Rogoff, B. (1992) Sociocultural processes of creative planning in children's playcrafting. In P. Light and G. Butterworth (eds) *Context and Cognition: Ways of Learning and Knowing.* Hemel Hempstead: Harvester-Wheatsheaf.

Bakhtin, M. (1986) In C. Emerson and M. Holquist (eds) *Speech Genres and Other Late Essays.* Austin: University of Texas Press.

Barbieri, M. and Light, P. (1992) Interaction, gender and performance on a computer-based task. *Learning and Instruction* 2, 199–213.

Barnes, D. (1992) The role of talk in learning. In K. Norman (ed.) *Thinking Voices.* London: Hodder & Stoughton.

Barnes, D. and Todd, F. (1977) *Communication and Learning in Small Groups.* London: Routledge & Kegan Paul.

Bell, N., Grossen, M. and Perret-Clermont, A-N. (1985) Sociocognitive conflict and intellectual growth. In M.W. Berkowitz (ed.) *Peer Conflict and Psychological Growth (New Directions in Child Development no.29).* San Francisco: Jossey-Bass.

Berrill, D. (1991) Exploring underlying assumptions: Small group work of university undergraduates. *Educational Review* 43 (2), 143–57.

Biggs, A. P. and Edwards, V. (1994) I treat them all the same: Teacher–pupil talk in multi-ethnic classrooms. In D. Graddol, J. Maybin and B. Stierer (eds) *Researching Language and Literacy in Social Context.* Clevedon: Multilingual Matters.

Billig, M., Condor, S., Edwards, D., Gane, M., Middleton, D. and Radley, A. (1988) *Ideological Dilemmas: A Social Psychology of Everyday Thinking.* London: Sage.

Blaye, A., Light, P., Joiner R. and Sheldon, S. (1991) Collaboration as facilitator of planning and problem-solving on a computer-based task. *British Journal of Developmental Psychology* 9, 471–83.

Bloome, D. (1993) Necessary indeterminacy and the microethnographic study of reading as a social process. *Journal of Research in Reading* 16 (2), 98–111.

Brah, A. and Minhas, R. (1988) Structural racism or cultural difference: Schooling for Asian girls. In M. Woodhouse and A. McGrath (eds) *Family, School and Society.* London: Hodder & Stoughton.

Brierley, L., Cassar, I., Loader, P., Norman, K., Shantry, I., Wolfe, S. and Wood, D.

(1992) No, we ask you questions. In K. Norman (ed.) *Thinking Voices: The Work of the National Oracy Project*. London: Hodder & Stoughton.

Brooks, G., Latham, J. and Rex, A. (1986) *Developing Oral Skills*. London: Heinemann.

Brown, G. and Wragg, E. C. (1993) *Questioning*. London: Routledge.

Brown, A. and Palincsar A. S. (1989) Guided, cooperative learning and individual knowledge acquisition. In L. Resnick (ed.) *Knowing, Learning and Instruction*. New York: Lawrence Erlbaum.

Bruner, J. S. (1978) The role of dialogue in language acquisition. In A. Sinclair, R. Jarvella and W. Levelt (eds) *The Child's Conception of Language*. New York: Springer-Verlag.

— (1985) Vygotsky: A historical and conceptual perspective. In J. Wertsch (ed.) *Culture, Communication and Cognition: Vygotskian Perspectives*. Cambridge: Cambridge University Press.

— (1986) *Actual Minds, Possible Worlds*. London: Harvard University Press.

— (1990) *Acts of Meaning*. London: Harvard University Press.

Clarke, K. (1991) *Primary Education — A Statement by the Secretary of State for Education and Science*. London: DES.

Cohen, S. (1973) *Folk Devils and Moral Panics: The Creation of Mods and Rockers*. London: Paladin.

Cole, M. (1985) The Zone of Proximal Development: Where culture and cognition create each other. In J. V. Wertsch. (1985) (ed.) *Culture, Communication and Cognition: Vygotskian Perspectives*. Cambridge: Cambridge University Press.

Cole, M. and Means, B. (1981) *Comparative Studies of How People Think: An Introduction*. Cambridge, MA: Harvard University Press.

Cole, M. and Scribner, S. (1974) *Culture and Thought*. New York: Wiley.

Coll, C. and Onrubia, J. (1994) Temporal dimensions and interactive processes in teaching-learning activities: A Theoretical and Methodological Challenge. In N. Mercer and C. Coll (eds) *Explorations in Socio-cultural Studies Vol.3: Teaching, Learning and Interaction*. Madrid: Infancia y Aprendizaje.

Croll, P. (1986) *Systematic Classroom Observation*. Lewes, Sussex: The Falmer Press.

Dawes, L. (1993) Special report: Talking points. *Junior Education*, February 1993.

Dawes, L., Mercer, N. and Fisher, E. (1992) The quality of talk at the computer. *Language and Learning*, October 1992.

Denscombe, M. (1985) *Classroom Control: A Sociological Perspective.* London: Allen & Unwin.

Dillon, J. T. (1982) The multidisciplinary study of questioning. *Journal of Educational Psychology* 74, 147–65.

— (1988) (ed.) *Questioning and Teaching: A Manual of Practice*. London: Croom Helm.

Doise, W. and Mugny, G. (1984) *The Social Development of Intellect*. Oxford: Pergamon Press.

Donaldson, M. (1978) *Children's Minds*. London: Fontana.

— (1992) *Human Minds*. London: Allen Lane.

Drew, P. and Heritage, J. (1992) (eds) *Talk at Work: Interaction in Institutional Settings*. Cambridge: Cambridge University Press.

Edwards, A. D. (1992) Teacher talk and pupil competence. In K. Norman (ed.)

Thinking Voices: The Work of the National Oracy Project. London: Hodder & Stoughton.

Edwards, D. (in press) Towards a discursive psychology of classroom education. In C. Coll (ed.) *Classroom Discourse.* Madrid: Infancia y Aprendizaje.

Edwards, A. D. and Westgate, D. (1987) *Investigating Classroom Talk.* London: The Falmer Press.

Edwards, D. and Mercer, N. (1987) *Common Knowledge: The Development of Understanding in the Classroom.* London: Methuen/Routledge.

Edwards, D. and Potter, J. (1992) *Discursive Psychology.* London: Sage.

Einstein, A. (1968) Letter to J. Hadamard. In B. Ghiselin (ed.) *The Creative Process.* Mentor: New York.

Elbers, E. (1991) The development of competence in its social context. *Educational Psychology Review* 3 (2), 73–93.

Elliot, J. (1991) *Action Research for Educational Change.* Milton Keynes: Open University Press.

Ellis, S. and Rogoff, B. (1986) Problem-solving in children's management of instruction. In E. Mueller and C. Cooper (eds) *Process and Outcome in Peer Relationhips.* San Diego: Academic Press.

Engestrom, Y. (1991) Activity theory and individual and social transformation. *Activity Theory* 7–8, 6–17.

Fisher, E. (1993) Distinctive features of pupil–pupil classroom talk and their relationship to learning: How discursive exploration might be encouraged. *Language and Education* 7 (4), 239–57.

Fletcher, B. (1985) Group and individual learning of junior school children on a microcomputer-based task. *Educational Review* 37, 251–61.

Gall, M. D. (1970) The use of questioning in teaching. *Review of Educational Research* 40, 707–21.

Galton, M., Simon, B. and Croll, P. (1980) *Inside the Primary Classroom (the ORACLE Project).* London: Routledge & Kegan Paul.

Galton, M. and Williamson, J. (1992) *Group Work in the Primary Classroom.* London: Routledge.

Gipps, C. (1994) What we know about effective primary teaching. In J. Bourne (ed.) *Thinking Through Primary Practice.* London: Routledge.

Greenfield, P.M. (1984) A theory of the teacher in the learning activities of everyday life. In B. Rogoff and J. Lave (eds) *Everyday Cognition: Its Development in Social Context.* Cambridge, MA: Harvard University Press.

Gregory, E. (1993) What counts as reading in the early years' classroom? *British Journal of Educational Psychology* 63, 214–30.

Hammersley, M. (1993) On the teacher as researcher. In M. Hammersley (ed.) *Educational Research: Current Issues.* London: Paul Chapman with the Open University.

Hatano, G. and Inagaki, K. (1992) Desituating cognition through the construction of conceptual knowledge. In P. Light and G. Butterworth (eds) *Context and Cognition: Ways of Learning and Knowing.* Hemel Hempstead: Harvester-Wheatsheaf.

Heath, S.B.(1983) *Ways with Words: Language, Life and Work in Communities and Classrooms* (p. 84). Cambridge: Cambridge University Press.

Hoyles, C., Healy, L. and Pozzi, S. (1992) Interdependence and autonomy: aspects of groupwork with computers. *Learning and Instruction* 2, 239–57.

Hoyles, C., Sutherland, R. and Healy, I. (1990) Children talking in computer environments: New insights on the role of discussion in mathematics learning. In K. Durkin and B. Shine (eds) *Language and Mathematics Education*. Milton Keynes: Open University Press.

Hull, R. (1985) *The Language Gap*. London: Methuen.

Jayalakshmi, G. D. (1993) Video in the English curriculum of an Indian secondary school. Ph.D. thesis, The Open University.

Kemmis, S. (1993) Action research. In M. Hammersley (ed.) *Educational Research: Current Issues*. London: Paul Chapman with the Open University.

Lave, J. (1992) Word problems: A microcosm of theories of learning. In P. Light and G. Butterworth (eds) *Context and Cognition: Ways of Learning and Knowing*. Hemel Hempstead: Harvester-Wheatsheaf.

Lemke, J. L. (1990) *Talking Science: Language Learning and Values*. Norwood, NJ: Ablex.

Leont'ev, A. N. (1981) *Problems of the Development of Mind*. Moscow: Progress Publishers.

Levinson, S. (1992) Activity types and language. In P. Drew and J. Heritage (1992) (eds) *Talk at Work: Interaction in Institutional Settings*. Cambridge: Cambridge University Press.

Light, P. (1991) Peers, problem-solving and computers. *Golem* 3 (1), 2–6.

— (1993) Collaborative learning with computers. In P. Scrimshaw (ed.) *Language, Classrooms and Computers*. London: Routledge.

Light, P. and Glachan, M. (1985) Facilitation of problem-solving through peer interaction. *Educational Psychology* 5, 217–25.

Light, P. and Littleton, K. (1994) Cognitive approaches to group work. In P. Kutnick and C. Rogers (eds) *Groups in Schools*. London: Cassell.

Light, P., Littleton, K., Messer, D. and Joiner, R. (1994) Social and communicative processes in computer-based problem-solving. *European Journal of Psychology of Education* 9 (2), 93–110.

Light, P. and Perret-Clermont, A-N. (1989) Social context effects in learning and testing. In A. Gellatly, D. Rogers and J. Sloboda (eds) *Cognition and Social Worlds*. Oxford: Clarendon Press.

Lipman, M. (1970) *Philosophy for Children*. Montclair, NJ: Institute for the Advancement of Philosophy for Children.

Lyle, S. (1993) An investigation into ways in which children 'talk themselves into meaning'. *Language and Education* 7 (3), 181– 97.

Madeley, B. and Lautman, A. (1991) I like the way we learn. In *Talk and Learning 5–16: An In-Service Pack on Oracy for Teachers*. Milton Keynes: The Open University.

Martin, T. (1986) Leslie: A reading failure talks about failing. In N. Mercer (ed.)

Language and Literacy from an Educational Perspective: Volume 2, In Schools. Milton Keynes: Open University Press.

Marton, F. (1989) Towards a pedagogy of content. *Educational Psychologist* 24 (1), 1–23.

Maybin, J. (1994) Children's voices: Talk, knowledge and identity. In D. Graddol, J. Maybin and B. Stierer (eds) *Researching Language and Literacy in Social Context*. Clevedon: Multilingual Matters.

Maybin, J., Mercer, N. and Stierer, B. (1992) 'Scaffolding' learning in the classroom. In K. Norman (ed.) *Thinking Voices*. London: Hodder & Stoughton.

Mehan, H. (1979) *Learning Lessons: Social Organization in the Classroom*. Cambridge, MA: Harvard University Press.

Mercer, N. (1991) Learning through talk. In P535 *Talk and Learning 5–16*. Milton Keynes: The Open University.

— (1992) Culture, context and the construction of knowledge in the classroom. In P. Light and G. Butterworth (eds) *Context and Cognition: Ways of Learning and Knowing*. Hemel Hempstead: Harvester-Wheatsheaf.

— (1994a) Neo-Vygotskian theory and education. In B. Stierer and J. Maybin (eds) *Language, Literacy and Learning in Educational Practice*. Clevedon: Multilingual Matters.

— (1994b) The quality of talk in children's joint activity at the computer. *Journal of Computer Assisted Learning* 10, 24–32.

Mercer, N. and Fisher, E. (1993) How do teachers help children to learn? An analysis of teachers' interventions in computer-based activities. *Learning and Instruction* 2, 339–55.

Mercer, N, and Longman, J. (1992) Accounts and the development of shared understanding in Employment Training Interviews. *Text* 12 (1), 103–25.

Messer, D., Joiner, R., Light, P. and Littleton, K. (1993) Influences on the effectiveness of peer interaction: Children's level of cognitive development and the relative ability of partners. *Social Development* 2 (3), 279–94.

Middleton, D. and Edwards, D. (1990) (eds) *Collective Remembering*. London: Sage.

Moll, L. (1990) (ed.) *Vygotsky and Education: Instructional Implications and Applications of Socio-historical Psychology* . Cambridge: Cambridge University Press.

Munjanja, A. (1995) Unit 1: Learning from traditional education. In *Classroom Text and Discourse: A Practical Course on Language in Schools*, produced by the LITRAID Project. Harare, Zimbabwe: The Rotary Club.

Newman, D., Griffin, P. and Cole, M. (1989) *The Construction Zone*. Cambridge: Cambridge University Press.

Norman, K. (ed.) *Thinking Voices: The Work of the National Oracy Project*. London: Hodder & Stoughton.

Northedge, A. (1990) *The Good Study Guide*. Milton Keynes: The Open University.

— (in press) *Making Sense of Studying*. London: Macmillan.

Nunes, T., Schliemann, A. D. and Carraher, D. (1993) *Street Mathematics and School Mathematics*. Cambridge: Cambridge University Press.

O'Connor, T. (1983) Classroom humour (Unpublished B.Phil. thesis, Newcastle

University), as quoted in Edwards, A. D. and Westgate, D. (1987) *Investigating Classroom Talk* (pp. 96–97). London: The Falmer Press.

O'Hear, A. (1987) The importance of traditional learning. *British Journal of Educational Studies* 35 (2), pp. 102–14.

Open University (1989) P537 *Developing Literacy and Numeracy*. Milton Keynes: Open University.

— (1991a) *Talk and Learning 5–16: An In-Service Pack on Oracy for Teachers*. Milton Keynes: The Open University.

— (1991b) EH232 *Computers and Learning*. Milton Keynes: The Open University.

Palincsar, A.M. (1986) The role of dialogue in providing scaffolded instruction. *Educational Psychologist* 21 (1&2), 73–98.

Paradise, R. (1993) 'Passivity' in social context: Mazahua mother–child interaction. Paper presented at the seminar on Co-operation and Social Context in Adult–child and Child–child Interaction at the University of Utrecht, November 1993.

Pearson, P. (1985) Changing the face of reading comprehension instruction. *The Reading Teacher* 38 (8), 724–38.

Philips, S. (1972) Participant structures and communicative competence. In C. Cazden, V. John and D. Hymes (eds) *The Functions of Language in the Classroom*. New York: Teachers College Press.

Phillips, T. (1990) Structuring talk for exploratory talk. In D. Wray (ed.) *Talking and Listening*. London: Scholastic.

— (1992) Why? The neglected question in planning for small group work. In K. Norman (ed.) *Thinking Voices*. London: Hodder and Stoughton.

Piaget, J. (1926) *The Language and Thought of the Child*. New York: Harcourt Brace Jovanovich.

— (1970) *The Science of Education and the Psychology of the Child*. New York: Viking Press.

— (1970) Piaget's theory. In P.H. Mussen (ed.) *Carmichael's Manual of Child Psychology*. New York: Wiley.

Pozzi, S., Healy, L. and Hoyles, C. (1993) Learning and interaction in groups with computers: When do ability and gender matter? *Social Development* 2 (3), 222–41.

Prentice, M. (1991) A community of enquiry. In *Talk and Learning 5–16: An In-Service Pack on Oracy for Teachers*. Milton Keynes: The Open University.

Rodrigues Rojo, R. (1994) Book reading in classroom interaction: From dialogue to monologue. In N. Mercer and C. Coll (eds) *Explorations of Sociocultural Studies Vol.3: Teaching, Learning and Interaction*. Madrid: Infancia y Aprendizaje.

Rogoff, B. (1990) *Apprenticeship in Thinking*. New York: Oxford University Press.

Rogoff, B. and Wertsch, J. (1984) Children's learning in the Zone of Proximal Development. In W. Damon (ed.) *New Directions in Child Development No.23*. San Francisco: Jossey Bass.

Rosen, H. (1993) How many genres in narrative? *Changing English* 1 (1), 179–91.

Sahni, U. (1992) Literacy for empowerment. Paper presented at the First Conference for Socio-cultural Research: A research agenda for educational and cultural change. Universidad Complutense de Madrid, Spain, October 1992.

Säljö, R. (1992) Human growth and the complex society: Notes on the monocultural bias in theories of learning. *Cultural Dynamics* 5 (1), 43–56.

Scrimshaw, P. (1993) (ed.) *Language, Classrooms and Computers*. London: Routledge.

Scruton, R. (1987) Expressionist education. *Oxford Review of Education* 13 (1), 39–44.

Sheeran, Y. and Barnes, D. (1991) *School Writing: Discovering the Ground Rules*. Milton Keynes: Open University Press.

— (1992) Oracy and genre. In K. Norman (ed.) *Thinking Voices*. London: Hodder and Stoughton.

Silcock, P. (1993) Towards a new progressivism in primary school education. *Educational Studies* 19 (1), 107–21.

Sinclair, J. and Coulthard, M. (1975) *Towards an Analysis of Discourse: The English used by Teachers and Pupils*. Oxford: Oxford University Press.

Steel, D. (1991) Granny's garden. In *Talk and Learning 5–16: An In-Service Pack on Oracy for Teachers*. Milton Keynes: The Open University.

Sutherland, P. (1992) *Cognitive Development Today: Piaget and his Critics*. London: Paul Chapman.

Swales, J. (1990) *Genre Analysis: English in Academic and Research Settings*. Cambridge: Cambridge University Press.

Swann, J. (1992) *Girls, Boys and Language*. London: Blackwell.

— (1994) What do we do about gender? In B. Stierer and J. Maybin (eds) *Language, Literacy and Learning in Educational Practice*. Clevedon: Multilingual Matters.

Talk Workshop Group (1982) *Becoming Our Own Experts: Studies of Language and Learning made by the Talk Workshop Group at Vauxhall Manor School, 1974–1979*. London: Talk Workshop Group.

Tharp, R. and Gallimore, R. (1990) A theory of teaching as assisted performance. In P. Light, S. Sheldon and M. Woodhead (eds) *Learning to Think: Child Development in Social Context 2*. London: Routledge.

Van Ness, H. (1982) Social control and social organization in an Athabaskan classroom: A micro-ethnography of getting ready for reading. In H. Tueba, G. Guthrie and K. Au (eds) *Culture in the Bilingual Classroom*. Rowley, MA: Newbury House.

Vygotsky, L.S. (1978) *Mind in Society*. London: Harvard University Press.

— (1962) *Thought and Language*. Cambridge, MA: MIT Press.

— (1934) cited in Wertsch, J.V. (1985) *Vygotsky and the Social Formation of Mind* (p. 71). Cambridge, MA: Harvard University Press.

— (1969) Thinking and speech. In R. Rieber and A. Carton (eds) *The Collected Works of L.S. Vygotsky, Vol.1: Problems of General Psychology*. New York: Plenum.

Wegerif, R. (1994) Educational Software and the Quality of Children's Talk. *Centre for Language and Communications Occasional Papers No. 40*. Milton Keynes: The Open University.

Wells, G. (1986) *The Meaning Makers* (Chapter 8). London: Hodder & Stoughton.

— (1992) The centrality of talk in education. In K. Norman (ed.) *Thinking Voices: The Work of the National Oracy Project*. London: Hodder & Stoughton.

— (1994) The complementary contributions of Halliday and Vygotsky to a language-based theory of learning. *Linguistics and Education* 6 (1), 41–90.

Wertsch, J. V. (1985) (ed.) *Culture, Communication and Cognition: Vygotskian Perspectives*. Cambridge: Cambridge University Press.

Westgate, D. and Corden, R. (1993) What we thought about things: Expectations, context and small group talk. *Language in Education* 7 (2), 115–26.

Willes, M. (1983) *Children into Pupils: A Study of Language in Early Schooling*. London: Routledge & Kegan Paul.

Wood, D. (1986) Aspects of teaching and learning. In M. Richards and P. Light (eds) *Children of Social Worlds* Cambridge: Polity Press.

— (1988) *How Children Think and Learn*. Oxford: Basil Blackwell.

— (1992) Teaching talk. In Norman, K. (ed.) *Thinking Voices: The Work of the National Oracy Project*. London: Hodder & Stoughton.

Wood, D., Bruner, J. and Ross, G. (1976) The role of tutoring in problem-solving. *Journal of Child Psychology and Child Psychiatry* 17, 89–100.

Index

131